For Dad
1948-2002
xx

I would like to thank the following people:

Heather Sneddon for constant encouragement, love and hot food (keep it coming!)

Phil Carter for taking time out of his heavy work schedule to read the first drafts

and, of course, thanks to TMG, without whom what you are about to read would not exist.

Cutting it Out

A Journey through Psychotherapy and Self-Harm

Carolyn Smith

Foreword by Maggie Turp

Jessica Kingsley Publishers
London and Philadelphia

First published in 2006
by Jessica Kingsley Publishers
116 Pentonville Road
London N1 9JB, UK
and
400 Market Street, Suite 400
Philadelphia, PA 19106, USA

www.jkp.com

Copyright © Carolyn Smith 2006
Foreword copyright © Maggie Turp 2006

Printed digitally since 2010

Library of Congress Cataloging in Publication Data
Smith, Carolyn, 1975-
   Cutting it out : a journey through psychotherapy and self-harm / Carolyn Smith ;
foreword by Maggie Turp.-- 1st American pbk. ed.
      p. cm.
   ISBN-13: 978-1-84310-266-3 (pbk. : alk. paper)
   ISBN-10: 1-84310-266-8 (pbk. : alk. paper) 1. Smith, Carolyn, 1975---Health. 2.
Self-injurious behavior--Patients--England--Biography. 3. Self-mutilation--Patients--
England--Biography. 4. Psychotherapy. I. Title.
   RC552.S4S63 2006
   362.196'8582'0092--dc22

                                  2005024694

British Library Cataloguing in Publication Data
A CIP catalogue record for this book is available from the British Library

ISBN 978 1 84310 266 3

Contents

Foreword by Maggie Turp 9

1. Mind the gap 11

2. Sweet rebellion 19

3. The traveller 21

4. Can you keep a secret? 27

5. Is it a bird? 31

6. Rituals and legends 34

7. Let's face the music 41

8. Treacle Tuesday 46

9. Bedrooms and nests 52

10. Well trained 57

11. Dream on 61

12. Timber! 63

13. Anthropomorphic adventures 67

14. Ejected 73

15. An understanding 78

16. Reflections 84

17. Operation Bin 86

18. Silent scrawl 91

19. Childish interpretations 93

20. Rescue me 99

21. A break too many 105

22. Fruit bowl stuff 114

23. All change 122

Further information and support 129

Foreword

Self-harm, in particular self-injury, has become an issue of pressing concern in recent years. Among young people in particular, it seems to be on the increase, seems to be a preferred way of expressing distress and coping with life's exigencies. This situation has resulted in a substantial literature on the subject – on the one hand books and papers written by therapeutic practitioners, on the other books and websites created by and for individuals who self-harm.

This book, an intimate and engaging account presented in the form of a novel, is a unique and important contribution to this literature. Eschewing sensationalism, the author offers a thoughtful and emotionally authentic account of her struggle with the compulsion to cut herself and a parallel compulsion to 'stalk' her psychotherapist. The story is set against the vividly and often humorously evoked backdrop of day-to-day life and work, and the relationships with her flatmate 'Kathryn', with her mother and with her recently deceased father.

The book is unusual in that – as the title suggests – it has at its centre the experience of psychotherapy described from the patient's point of view. The author records what transpires between herself and her psychotherapist and, beyond that, succeeds in communicating the feeling and the texture of the psychotherapy sessions, something that is very difficult to put into words. I was particularly interested in the account of the evolving relationship between client and psychotherapist and in the author's musings – never less than forthright – on some of her therapist's interventions ('She settles in for a long therapist explanation ...')! There is an enormous amount here to think about and to learn from, both for psychoanalytic practitioners and for practitioners employing other theoretical frameworks.

The eminent psychoanalyst Wilfred Bion emphasised that we find it hard to tolerate not knowing. Faced with distress and uncertainty, we find ourselves drawn towards premature conclusions and ill-founded generalisations that side-step the complexity of human experience and human behaviour. As I have noted elsewhere, some contributions to the self-harm literature fall into this trap and are marred by an overzealous search for 'one-size-fits-all' explanations of self-harming behaviour.

The narrative here is a salutary lesson in resisting such tendencies. It shows us the necessity and the value of living with uncertainty. The author's account shows clearly that stereotyped images and explanations of self-harm are both inaccurate and unhelpful. She has not been sexually abused; she has not been abused or neglected in her family; she has not been in foster care or in prison. In her moving and sometimes painfully honest account, she insists on describing things as they seem to her to be, never reaching for an easy explanation. We live with her through her painful uncertainty. Through therapy, glimpses of understanding emerge, connections begin to be made, but still there is much that remains unclear.

Readers who are considering seeking psychotherapy but hesitating, wondering what it might be like, are likely to find this book immensely helpful. Readers who are practitioners will know that good and thoughtful accounts of the therapeutic journey described from the patient's side of the equation are rarer than gold dust. For both groups, there is much to enjoy, value and mull over in this excellent book.

Dr Maggie Turp, C. Psychol, UKCP
Psychoanalytic Psychotherapist and author of
Hidden Self-Harm: Narratives from Psychotherapy

Chapter 1
Mind the gap

Macabre patterns in the water. Poisoned smoke.
The sting of a new cut.
Calming, peaceful and secretive.

The wind howls around and I pull my jacket tighter round my body. Sitting on the back of the bench with my feet on the seat, my hands shred a leaf pulled from a nearby bush and I watch the commuters flood up in waves from the train station. Nobody looks at me. Too busy. Too hassled. Too cold. Clutching onto bags and papers, their raincoats blow about their legs, they disperse into the streets, scuttling home to warm rooms, behind closed curtains, with potted plants and a flashing TV. Doors open and shut, shafts of other people's lives flood the pavements, but only for a second, then it's dark again.

The sky is dusk blue and the moon peers down as again I am alone. It's a great view from my bench. To the right, beyond the railway line, lights of the city appear between the trees, a theatre curtain, half open, offering a glimpse of a glittering show. Too far away to see the performers or understand the plot, but you feel a part of it all the same. In front of the bench is a line of shops running down to the train station. One of the shops is boarded up and is home only to a semi-talented graffiti artist and a pigeon that is peering back at me. Above each shop are flats with more curtains blocking the view to a stranger's world. A small boy appears from a black door, holding his football, slamming the door behind him. The pigeon visibly jumps and flies away to the safety of a tree. Above, a face briefly appears through a pair of yellowing grey curtains. The boy gives a quick wave and rushes off, the way of the commuters, the sound of his bouncing ball growing quieter.

To the left, where the boy is disappearing round a corner, lies a mass of North London streets, the road nearest lined with cars, large Victorian houses and tall trees. The leaves from the trees are beginning to form their annual orange carpet on the pavements. The wind catches some of them and they flutter up, as if trying to reach their branches again, but fail and float gently back to ground.

The number of doorbells suggests most of the houses have been turned into flats, one on each floor. One of the houses has a blue door, newly painted, with chrome numbers telling everyone that it is number 57. There is a car parked outside with a registration number I know off by heart; the driver will be waiting to see me at seven o'clock in the ground floor flat of number 57. I look at my watch. A new batch of commuters troop towards me. I jump off the bench and join them, head across the road and stand outside number 57. The car is parked a little way further up the road, its wheels pointing left, as if the parker had lost patience. The security light beams on as I open the gate and walk up the short path. The neighbour's cat mews a hello and stares at me. It is a scruffy little thing with a head too big for its body and fur that needs brushing. I tickle it behind its ears then wipe the greasy feeling on my jeans. I press the bell for Flat 1 and wait. The cat waits too. After a moment, a voice crackles 'Hello'. I reply in kind, a buzz sounds and I push open the door. The cat stays on the fence staring at me as I close the door on it and the wind outside.

The hallway is warm but dark, until I push the white light switch, then it jumps into brightness. I blink. Familiar cream walls and a cream carpet, thick and newly laid, welcome me. There are wooden shelves holding a red flowering plant in a black pot and some mail waiting to be claimed. I scan the names on the envelopes but they are for people in the other flats, not number 1. Ahead of me there is a deep red door, and to the right, a staircase that I assume leads up to the other flats. Within seconds the blue door has opened and she greets me with a smile. I smile back, unable to maintain eye contact, and walk past her into flat number 1.

There are only two rooms that I go into in flat number 1; the rest are out of bounds. The door to one of these forbidden rooms is open and I glance in on my way past. A big leather chair with a high headrest sits behind, and to the left of, a white couch. There is a desk with a computer and shelves and shelves of books. I turn right and pass through the kitchen. There are cups waiting to be washed, an orange peel on a white plate and a silver kettle, recently boiled and steaming on the worktop. I walk across the cork-tiled floor to my destination. A small rug splashes colour on another cream carpet and the yellow walls are lit in different places by strategically placed lamps. Red curtains are pulled across the French windows and suddenly it feels like a long time since I saw the garden on the other side. A blank sheet of lined paper and a pen lie on the desk by her chair. There is no computer on this desk like in the other room, but instead a laptop sits neatly packed away in its black case in a corner. I sit on a suede couch facing the curtained windows and drop my jacket to the floor. I feel her walk in and hear the door close quietly. She sits in her chair behind me.

Silence.

My eyes follow the pattern of the curtains for a moment as I let my mind settle; even after a year I still get nervous about coming here. I close my eyes and see if I can hear her breathing. I can't; that unnerves me. Sometimes it's difficult to tell if she's there and I want to swing round and make sure she is concentrating on me and not writing out her shopping list on that blank piece of paper.

'So how have you been feeling after the last session?' she asks, her voice gentle. There's a hint of an Irish accent, but only just, only if you really listen.

'I've been OK, you know.' I unconsciously touch my wrist and pull down my shirt sleeve. 'I just get angry sometimes.'

'Angry with whom?' she probes, gently rocking back on her chair.

'Myself, no one else, just me,' I answer, very defensively. I started therapy a year ago because of my self-harm. I saw a counsellor at first whom I just didn't like. We didn't click, I didn't trust her. She reminded me of my mum and why would I want to talk to my mum about my secret inner world? I'd written her a note and said I wasn't coming back – the counsellor, not my mum. I didn't think she could cope with my cutting, she often looked appalled when I mentioned it, but that could have been my paranoia about it. She'd sent me a Christmas card wishing me well and saying that I had started to improve and my self-identity was beginning to shine through. I felt bad, but not bad enough to not send her a card back and start here at number 57 in January. I felt much more comfortable here straight away. She looked as though she could take a good shouting at and not fall over. She didn't remind me of my mother. She didn't flinch when I introduced myself with the sentence, 'I'm here because I'm a cutter.' I felt she needed to know from the outset and she was interested that my identity was first and foremost as a cutter, something I'd never really thought about until then.

'Where have you gone?' she asks, leaning forward in her chair so she can see my face, my eyes tight shut.

'I'm not sure,' I sigh. 'I think I'm just tired today.' I take a deep breath, smelling vanilla floating up from a small candle burning on a table across the room. The candle throws flickering light on to the bookshelf, illuminating titles I re-read every time I'm here.

'Did you cut?' She doesn't usually ask, but then I'm usually forthcoming in telling her when it happens.

'No,' I lie. A blatant lie, I'm not sure why, but I felt I had to. Sometimes it's just easier to lie than have to talk about the reasons why.

Silence.

She doesn't believe me.

'OK,' I sigh. 'I did, just a little, nothing bad.' I rub my wrist again. It still stings. She stays silent.

Count the scars. Don't let them disappear. If they disappear you won't be real, you won't exist. The sting keeps you alive, brings you back from the edge.

'It's been a long week,' she agrees, soothing me with her voice. Sometimes I want to sit and watch her as she talks; I so rarely see her face. 'You've been working really hard recently; you've been doing really well.'

I close my eyes and squeeze them shut. Sometimes it's too much. When I'm not here I ache to be here, but when I am, sometimes I just want to leave. This was one of those times.

My head wanders.

My dad died eight months ago. It never dawned on me how much I would miss him. I don't think it has even yet.

My mum was out visiting her parents, telling them how well they looked, and yes, she could get them some new pillow-cases next time she was in town.

He died alone. He'd just finished dusting. He was found in the toilet, like Elvis but without the glitz. It was Mother's Day. My mum had to phone my gran and tell her that her son was dead. On Mother's Day, imagine that. The day will never fade, it will never become just another Sunday. Mother's Day happens every year. My dad's death will happen every year.

'Stay with me,' she says, sensing I'm drifting into the place where I'm unreachable, 'Talk to me. Why are you tired?'

I let out a long sigh as my mind struggles back to the here and now. 'I feel exhausted. My mind never stops. Why won't it stop?' I rub the palm of my hand over my forehead.

'What did you just rub away?' she asks, 'What do you want to erase?'

The firemen had to break in through the toilet window to get my dad out. I swept the glass up the next day. There are two black, shadowy handprints on the lilac walls, where the fireman pulled himself through the broken window. I wish my mum would wipe them away; maybe she doesn't see them. I see them every time I visit the house. I don't like to shut the toilet door at her house anymore. If I do, I picture my dad there. A lasting memory I never really saw.

I shake my head. My mind won't connect with my mouth. There are no words to speak. Someone in the upstairs flat flushes a toilet and switches on some music. The rhythm of the drums keep time with the thudding in my head. I look at the ceiling.

'Sorry about them, they're students,' she says, by way of explanation. She sits silently again.

'I often wonder if it is annoying for you to sit there and know there are things in my head that refuse to come out,' I say, folding my arms.

No response.

'It's not that I don't want to say these things, but I'm not sure how to.' I close my eyes. 'Push me.'

I hear her write something on the paper.

'Push you where?' she asks, crossing her legs, a red shoe coming into my field of vision.

'Into the void,' I whisper. 'I can't go there on my own.'

The first phone call I got was from my brother to say Dad had collapsed. We told each other he'd be fine. I'd ring him later. The second phone call was my mum. No, he wasn't all right, she said. He's dead. DEAD. The words would reverberate around my mind for weeks. They'd echo in my heart for longer and plant themselves in my soul for ever.

'Tell me about the void,' her voice gently probing me for information.

'Its deep,' I say, my fingers playing with a button on my shirt. 'You can't see the bottom; it's too dark.'

'Where is this void?' Her chair creaks as she leans forward, trying to see into my mind.

'At the edge,' I say, closing my eyes and picturing the sheer drop. 'I sit on the edge, one foot on solid ground, the other dangling over the void.'

'Look into it for me,' she urges. 'What can you see?' Her voice is quiet now, not wanting to jolt me back.

I close my eyes, hands clinging to the side of the couch as if I might actually fall in. I can feel my heart beating fast against my chest, my breathing more urgent.

'It's too dark,' I say again, concentrating hard. 'It's such a mess, so chaotic, I can't tell what is what.'

'Like madness?' I hear her say, a long way off.

'Yeah,' I breathe, 'and part of me wants to be in there so badly, but the other part is scared. But I feel like it needs to be done. I need to separate all the swirling parts to understand it.'

'And you want me to push you?'

'I can't do it on my own.' My knuckles turn white as I grab tighter to the edge of the couch.

There is silence for a while as I try to tear my eyes away from the void. It's almost magnetic, but I know if I jump in I won't come out intact.

'I need to think about this,' she says, almost to herself. 'We need to think about how to make this safe for you.'

Her voice brings me back and I open my eyes and am pleased to see the red curtains once more. I leave number 57 and stand outside letting the wind blow away the session. I look at my watch and cross the road to wait for the bus. I'm meeting Kathryn, my flatmate, at the cinema. A new comedy has started and we both thought that would be a good way to start the weekend and forget about the session. I board the bus and watch the small, scruffy cat balancing on the fence post waiting for the next client at number 57.

Chapter 2
Sweet rebellion

M*y dad had been in and out of hospital lots when I was a child.
Bad heart. As a child I used to think how I would react if he died.
This time it was real. I had no time to think about reaction. I sobbed. I
dropped to my knees in disbelief. It was never really supposed to
happen.*

The film is a bit boring and my mind keeps wandering.
Kathryn has plied me with chocolates and is now holding a
tub of popcorn under my nose, but my head still won't stay in
the moment.

*That's not why I cut myself. I was doing that for at least a year before
my dad died. Maybe I was preparing myself. But I think I was
perhaps psycho already. That's how it feels. I'm mad, crazy. I just
know how to hide it really well.*

We finish the popcorn and I laugh out loud for the first time
since the film started, not because the comedy has finally
come good, but because Kathryn has produced another bag of
sweets. I look at her. She just raises her eyebrows as if it is
normal to eat our way through the whole snack counter in the
first hour of a film. We loudly unwrap a hard-boiled sweet
each and have our normal competition of who can suck the

sweet the longest without chewing. Sounds easier than it is and has entertained us through many a rubbish film.

I remember the first time I cut. I think everyone remembers their first time. I'd always been the type of child to hold in their anger and would throw things around my room when I was on my own. I go back to visit now and count the holes in the walls I've made along the way to growing up and leaving the nest. But hurting a wall is very different from hurting yourself and I was scared after the first time. It felt like progressing to Level Two on a computer game and not really understanding the rules.

Then Kathryn does something I've not done since I was 13. She unwraps a sweet and throws it over the balcony.

I splutter my drink into my lap and whisper, 'They're hard boiled, you daft cow! You've probably just killed someone.'

We both peer over the balcony.

'Your eyes were glazing over,' she whispers back. 'I thought you needed waking up.'

'And did the poor guy below need waking up?'

She looks at me and we both get the giggles. The person behind us taps Kathryn on the shoulder and asks us to be quiet; we think it is time to leave. We grab our coats and head out onto the bustling street outside. We burst into laughter and head for the nearest pub. Sometimes it is nice to know I have a real life to cling on to. Kathryn ruffles my hair as if reading my mind and declares, 'You owe me one, it's your round!'

Who am I to argue?

Chapter 3
The traveller

So, what shall we do today?
You want to play our game again?
Do you? Do you? Do you? Do you?

I sit on my bedroom carpet with my legs crossed. I rock gently, my eyes tight shut.

'Leave me alone,' my voice barely a whisper. 'Just leave me alone.' I'd woken with a hangover after a raucous night with Kathryn and now my mind is kicking me whilst I am down.

My room is untidy. The sort of untidy that would make my mum raise her eyebrows and shake her head. A blanket box can barely be seen under the heap of jeans, t-shirts and discarded socks. By my bed a pile of books and newspapers is used as a handy table for three empty mugs of tea and a plate of toast crumbs. By the side of the 'table' is a box of tissues and underneath the first layer of tissues is my secret stash of razor blades. I imagine it to be similar to that of an alcoholic who hides his bottles of gin around the house. In the airing cupboard, underneath the bottle of talc no one uses is another stash of blades. In the bathroom cabinet is a box of moisturiser; shake the box and you'll hear another stash rattling. In my wallet, inside the book of stamps, is another blade…just in case. It makes me feel safe. Never too far away from a release. Our cat crawls out from underneath my bed and mews a hello. I stroke him and promise him food, but my head hasn't finished yet.

I THINK WE SHOULD PLAY.
YOU KNOW YOU NEED TO.
YOU KNOW YOU HAVE TO.
WHY FIGHT IT WHEN YOU KNOW WHAT YOU WANT TO DO?

I take deep breaths and stand up. I have already showered and eaten breakfast, trying to shake off my hangover. I pull on my jeans and look for the least creased T-shirt in my drawer. I'm tired and don't have the energy to be in the real world today. I'm ready and I let myself be taken over by the other side of me. The side that lives in the void.

I walk past the living room. I hear Kathryn listening to a loud Saturday morning TV show. I say 'Bye' quietly, too quietly so she doesn't hear and won't ask me where I'm going. The cat sees me zipping up my jacket and bounds down the stairs in the hope of having an adventure with me.

'You don't go out the front,' I tell him, and shoo him back inside. I pull the door closed gently and head off towards the bus stop.

The day is fresh and cold, with a crisp blue sky. My breath curls out in front of me, like smoke, and I suddenly want a cigarette. An urge that is over as soon as it starts, but I'm taken aback. I stopped smoking the day my dad died, and have not thought of cigarettes since. I remember the time, when I still lived in Leeds, when my dad turned up at my flat un-announced. I answered the door cigarette in hand. My dad never flinched, but I quickly threw the cigarette, still alight, down the back of a bookshelf. I had never told my parents I smoked; they would have been too disappointed.

Cutting is like smoking, but oh, so much harder to stop.
I feel an ache inside me if I deny myself the time to cut.
I need it. I need it for so many reasons.
Maybe I enjoy it.
I know many people who won't stop smoking because they enjoy it. It's
their crutch. Cutting is mine and I defensively defend it.

I wonder if my therapist smokes. I smile and think, no. I can't picture her smoking, the smoke would mask her face. I sit on the narrow seat at the bus stop and think of her face. Sometimes I have to concentrate for a long time until I see her. I think about her eyes, so blue, so heart-stoppingly blue. Sometimes I think therapy on tap would be such a good thing. Whenever thirst hits you, just turn the tap and there she'd be. Or bottle it and carry it round for those awkward family parties, when a dose of therapy might just help you through the evening. And help some of the others, come to think of it, but they'd have to find their own tap. Mine isn't for sharing.

A bus pulls up and I board, flashing my pass to a driver who barely acknowledges me. I take a seat on the upper deck and stare out of the window. A pregnant woman runs up to the door as the bus driver pulls away. She gestures rudely at him, and rubs her stomach.

I FEEL BETTER NOW.
I FEEL BETTER NOW I'M ON MY WAY.
LOOKING. SEARCHING. GETTING CLOSER.
ISN'T THIS EXCITING?
ARE WE THERE YET?

I sit there, watching the houses and shops and people and traffic moving by below me. My head is working out all the different ways I can travel to get to my destination. I don't want to get there too quickly. I like the travelling, the moving. I like the anticipation. Sitting on a bus is passive; it allows me to pretend I'm not doing anything wrong. I'm just on a bus.

The journey is going quite well until the traffic grinds to a halt and in the distance I can see the fluorescent vests of workmen and the yellow flashing lights of digger trucks. I fish out my headphones from the inside pocket of my jacket and switch on my personal CD player. I do this a lot; not only does it keep the world away, but it drowns out the sound of my mind:

ARE WE THERE YET?
WHY HAVE WE STOPPED?
WHERE IS...

'She's got a ticket to ri-i-ide, she's got a ticket to ride, and she don't care...'

I rest my head on the back of the seat and watch the wispy white clouds floating across the sky, disappearing behind blocks of flats, appearing at the other side a different fluffy shape. I can feel the voice banging against my forehead, but for now I can't hear it, but I always know it's there.

The bus crawls on, stopping at more traffic lights, letting pedestrians cross the road, at times just stopping for no reason. The streets of London start to get busier, as people begin their Saturday shopping, dragging small children behind them. After 45 minutes I press the bell to stop the bus and alight, suddenly being carried along by crowds of people. There are so many noises, so much to look at, but I'm focused and am not distracted from my mission. One more bus journey and I'll be there, then what I'm not sure, but I just know I have to be there.

COME ON, KEEP UP.
NEARLY THERE, OH WE'RE NEARLY THERE.
ISN'T THIS EXCITING?

I listen and can't help but get carried away with its enthusiasm, but up till now I've managed to stay in control. Yes, I'm giving it what it wants, but I'm in control. I can stop whenever I want.

NO, YOU CAN'T, DON'T LIE TO YOURSELF.
YOU'RE GOING THERE NOW BECAUSE YOU HAVE TO. DON'T BLAME IT ON ME.
YOU NEED...

I turn my music up and drown the voice out once more. The next bus arrives and I sit on the back seat downstairs. I'll be getting off soon and I can feel the adrenalin beating fast in anticipation. When I get off the bus I know the music will be switched off and it'll be allowed to take over. Then I can blame it. It won't be my fault.

I found out where she lived on the internet. A few simple searches in the right places and I have an address, a date of birth and middle name. I can't explain why I need all this information. I just do. It's an impulse I have to act on.

'You're filling a gap.' I suddenly hear my therapist's voice in my head and in the pit of my stomach I know she is saying the truth, but I still don't understand.

I'm now standing at the end of her road.

The music switches off, as does my capacity to act with consequences in mind.

When I was little I used to play on my own a lot. There was some wasteland at the end of our road and I would ride my bike round and round, pretending to be in a race full of other cyclists, but really it was just me. A shy child, I hated to see other people heading my way; this was my wasteland and it annoyed me when other people spoiled my fantasy world.

Children are allowed a fantasy world, but as an adult my fantasy world was something I had no control of. As a child you'd get called in for tea and you'd be back in the real world, having your cold beef sandwiches and pickle. As an adult no one calls you in for tea, no one calls you back from your fantasy world. Everyone has fantasies, whether it's about winning the lottery or becoming an astronaut, but do you know where your fantasy ends and the real world kicks in? Are you scared that the fantasy world might end, that you'll be left naked, feeling the raw biting cold of reality? I am. My fantasies are like a warm duvet, wrapped tightly around me, buffering me from the world. A cocoon. Will I ever emerge out the other side, a beautiful butterfly? Not here, not right now, I'm too lost inside my duvet. I'll have two new cuts in the morning.

Chapter 4

Can you keep a secret?

'You look upset,' she says, as I sit on the couch and fidget uncomfortably.

My session started ten minutes ago and I have yet to speak. If I don't open my mouth then I don't have to tell her what happened on Saturday.

She tries again. 'You seem agitated; do you want to tell me about it?'

I want to squeeze myself into a ball and disappear in a puff of smoke, but I don't tell her this.

'No,' is all I say.

She lets me stew in silence for a few minutes longer. And then, 'Tell me about what's happened for you since our last session.'

I look at the clock that sits on the table opposite me. Fifteen minutes I've wasted in silence. I breathe in deeply.

'Nothing really. I've not been good. It's been hard to keep things real.'

'Doesn't sounds like 'nothing really' to me,' she replies.

I hold my head in my hands. 'I don't know, I don't know.' I scratch my nails down my forehead.

'Come on,' she says quietly. 'Try and bring it in here; it's safe to do that, you know.'

DON'T YOU TELL HER WHAT YOU DID. DON'T YOU DARE. SHE WON'T UNDERSTAND WHY YOU DID IT. SHE DOESN'T NEED TO KNOW. SHOW HER YOUR NEW CUTS, TALK ABOUT THOSE INSTEAD.

I stare at the pictures on the office walls. One of a nude woman looks like a Matisse print but it's not; there is a signature in the bottom right hand corner, but I can't quite make out the name. To my left there are black and white photos in silver frames. I wonder if she took them on a distant holiday away from patients like me.

'I can see whatever happened was upsetting and that you found it hard to deal with.' She refers to my arms. I'm wearing short sleeves.

'Yes,' I agree, tracing the line of the cuts with my index finger, 'I was angry with myself. The cutting was about anger this time.'

I sit motionless, not wanting her to enquire into where this anger came from. If I sit still enough she might forget about me. I stare at the vase of flowers that sits on the table next to the clock. I suddenly want to climb inside the flower and close the petals around me.

'And why do you think you were so angry? What has been going on?'

I peek out from behind the petals.

NO NO NO NO. DON'T TELL HER. THINGS WILL HAVE TO CHANGE IF YOU TELL HER. TELL HER AND SHE'LL HATE YOU TOO.

'I can't say, I'm not allowed to say. I'm not ready to bring that in here yet,' I splutter, and promptly fold the flower petals back round my head.

I can hear her mind working. I frustrate her, I can tell.

'It sounds important. Can you tell me if it was something you did or something you thought?' She tries to reel me in, stop me from closing myself off completely.

'Both,' I say, my voice muffled from the petals around my face.

I push away one of the petals and gaze at the clock. Ten minutes left; how can I start talking about it with only ten minutes left? Perhaps if I stare at it long enough and think hard enough I can stop the hands from going around, stop time, have forever with this person who seems to want to help me.

'I'm not sure I dare tell you what happened,' I try, pushing another petal away, trying to free myself. 'I'm scared of what you will think of me, what you will do if I tell you these things, what will happen when it's all out in the open. You'll hate me if I tell you,' I splutter, all in one breath.

OF COURSE SHE'LL HATE YOU.
WE HAVE TO KEEP THIS SECRET.
NO ONE ELSE WILL UNDERSTAND.

She stays quiet for what seems like a long time. I wonder what she's thinking. Is she thinking she hates me already? Is she thinking how to make me feel better? Is she thinking about her weekend? I want to turn round and see the look on her face, watch her face for clues.

'I wish you could read my mind,' I say finally. 'I just wish you could open my mind and see what is there. I don't want to speak it out loud.' I used to believe that my mum could read my mind when I was little. If I'd done something naughty, like feeding the dog jam, then I didn't have to say anything because she already knew. She didn't read my mind, obviously, and the dog got very fat on jam and I never got told off. To my mum I was a good girl, always a good girl. A quiet girl, no tantrums, no name-calling. So quiet. Too quiet. But quiet doesn't always mean good; sometimes it means scared.

'Perhaps you could think about writing it down,' she suggests, 'if you think that might help you bring it in here. It does sound important.'

I think about writing it down, about watching her face as she reads it. I was about to reply when she says those dreaded words.

'Well, it's time.'

I sigh a little too loudly and stand up. I watch her walk out of the office and hold open the front door for me. I nod a goodbye and walk out into the streets of North London again. North London, a great place to get lost in, to be totally anonymous. I came to London three years ago. I'd finished university and moved back to my parents' house. It was never going to work. My mum would wait up for me and ask me where I'd been. I'd left home at 17; I wasn't used to all the questions. I moved to London not long after. My mum thought it was because I'd got a job, which I had, but really it was because London is 200 miles away from Leeds, where my mum still lives. No one waits up for me anymore; I can do what I like, no responsibilities. I smile and head for the pub.

Chapter 5
Is it a bird?

Staggering across the pavement I lean against a wall and look down the dimly lit street. The lamp posts fight for their space with overgrown trees, that dangle their branches in front of the light.

I hiccup, run my fingers though my hair and breathe deeply. My head spins and I hold onto the wall more tightly. Car headlights turn the corner and I try to shrink myself into the shadow. I watch the car go past the house with the green front door, number 41. The blinds at each window are fully closed, not showing if there are lights on behind, if anyone is at home.

I push myself away from the wall and sidle my way up closer to the house. I lean against a tree and watch the upstairs window.

A voice in my head clambers its way to the front and asks, 'What are you doing here again?'

I slap my forehead, knocking the voice back and refuse to answer that question tonight.

I stand at the edge of the path that leads up to number 41 and scan the street for the car I know so well. It's not there; perhaps you're not home yet. I look at my watch. The drink has made my eyes blurred and I think it is 11 o'clock, but it may be later, I'm not sure.

There is a sign on your door that says 'Beware of the Dog', or at least that's what I think it says. Something stops me from

going any closer and reading it properly. I suddenly realise
that the 'something' is me. Like a scene from a superhero
comic I blaze down from the sky and stand in front of myself,
my superhero cape flapping in the wind.

'What the hell do you think you're doing?' I ask myself,
loud and clear, the first superhero with a slight Yorkshire
accent. 'This is not good; this is actually really silly. This is
your therapist's house, for goodness sake! Go home.'

GO HOME? BUT I'VE ONLY JUST GOT HERE.

But I'm taken aback by my sudden awareness of where I am,
that I have no idea what I'm doing here. I feel myself returning
and the voice slides back into the void.

'Superhero Me' disappears, cape and all, and it's just me,
standing alone on a dark London street, too far from home
and suddenly quite scared. I take out my mobile phone and
dial her number, wanting to listen to her voice on the
answerphone. I sometimes do this, just to calm me.

'Thank you for calling the consulting rooms of...'

This time is different though. I'm waiting for the beep
and I'm not going to hang up.

*'...do leave a message and your call will be returned as soon as
possible.'*

Beep.

For a moment I don't know what to say but then I hear
myself telling the machine who I am and who I'm leaving a
message for.

'I'm somewhere I shouldn't be,' I slur, 'and it's dark and
cold and I'm scared. I shouldn't be here, I'm in trouble.'

I'm not sure how I end the one-way conversation, because
the next thing I know I'm sitting in a black cab on my way
home.

Kathryn is sitting at the top of the stairs when I finally manage to get my keys into the lock and stumble through the door.

'Where the hell have you been?' she says, her face turning into my mother's. 'I've been bloody worried. You could have told me you were going out after therapy.'

'You've waited up for me?' I say trying to sound oh so sober. 'You shouldn't wait up for me, I'm a good girl, you know.'

'Hey, I'm your best mate and if you're going out for a drinking session I think I should be allowed out too!'

She doesn't sound too angry and if I had been sober I would have heard a hint of worry in her voice. She knows me well enough that if I go drinking on my own something is wrong.

Chapter 6
Rituals and legends

Cross-legged in the middle of the floor, head hung low, eyes closed, breathing slow. I'm cross with myself for what I did last night.

In front of me, on the carpet, is my watch, a box of tissues, a razor blade.

There is one hour before Kathryn returns from her book group. She keeps asking me to go with her, but if I read a book I don't then feel the need to talk to a group of strangers about it, so I decline politely.

I pull a tissue from the box and lay it neatly on the floor.

I pick up the blade.

LET THE RITUAL COMMENCE.

The cat, sensing this is a private act, slides off the settee and leaves the room. It's not quite dark outside yet, but I've drawn the curtains. The school at the end of the road spews out its pupils, who whoop and shout as they climb into cars and are driven home to TV and computers. An angry song thumps from my stereo and I lean forward turning up the volume.

The voice in my head is clambering to be heard, but I just need some space, I need it to leave me alone. I look at the framed photo of my dad and the tears come, but so does the voice.

I HATE YOU, I HATE YOU, I HATE YOU!

Childish chanting, as if it can't think of anything more constructive to say. Wanting to push me over the edge, wanting to see the blood and feel pain. I put the blade down and hold my head.

'I don't want to do this,' I say, sobbing now.

LIAR! LIAR! LIAR!

And I know it's the truth. I want to cut, I want to see the pain, to take it out of my head. My flatmate is due home soon so I know I have to be 'normal' by the time she comes in. The crime scene needs to be cleared. I have to be making tea and laughing about her day and telling her I'm fine and did she manage to buy that sweater she wanted.

I'M LOOKING OVER THE EDGE OF THE VOID.
IT'S DARK AND DEEP.
DOWN THERE IS MADNESS.
I CAN FEEL IT PULLING ME CLOSER.
I WANT TO JUMP.

I shake my head violently. 'You're not pulling me in there, I don't want to go.'

My breathing is fast and I can't keep up with the voice in my head. It's saying too many things too fast. I pick up the blade. The voice begins to fade and the tears dry up as the blood begins to flow.

The last few children are leaving the school, dragging behind them their bags and scuffing their shoes on the ground. These are the few who don't want to rush home, for whom school is a refuge. Maybe one day they'll have their own void to look into too. For now mine was disappearing, being pushed farther back in my mind, to a safer place where I wouldn't fall down it just now.

Picking up the tissue I hold it tightly against my arm, the stinging soothing me back to reality. Deep breaths.

I turn the music off and walk to the kitchen, stopping to stroke the cat's head as he looks up at me with all-knowing eyes. I turn the tap on and let the cold water rinse over my arm. The water swirls pink as it disappears down the plughole. I wrap the blood-soaked tissue in some kitchen roll before throwing it in the bin. Covering my tracks is a natural instinct.

I flick the switch on the kettle and listen to the hiss whilst admiring the new marks on my arm. I'm strangely pleased and look forward to my next therapy session.

The kettle boils and I make myself a cup of tea, opening a packet of biscuits with my teeth. I sit at the kitchen table and look at my wrist. It hurts and I wonder how I can keep this hidden from people until it fades a little. I've tried wearing long sleeves, but I have the habit of rolling them up above my elbows anyway. I come to the conclusion that most people don't look at other people's arms. No one has ever mentioned my scars at work, at least not to my face.

I hear a key turning in the door. The door opens and Kathryn stamps in, shaking her umbrella outside and wiping her feet on the mat.

'Hey, you in?' she calls, throwing her coat over the radiator and walking up the stairs.

I take another look at my arm and answer her in a cheery voice.

'Yeah, mate, I'm in the kitchen. You fancy a brew? Kettle's just boiled.'

'Sure, thanks,' she replies, walking into the kitchen, carrying the cat who ambushed her on the stairs.

There is a story behind our cat. Well, not so much a story, more of a legend. When Kathryn and I moved into the flat it was a cat-free environment. We'd both said we didn't want pets, we were too young for such responsibilities. Kathryn wanted no ties, to be able to come and go as she pleased. She worked hard and played harder, a motto she used to shout at me as she left for another evening in the pub. I'd tighten my dressing gown cord and wave at her through the window, before drawing the curtains and getting out my current book. Life in the fast lane, that was us. Well, Kathryn at least. Depression leaving me with no inclination to claw my way out of the slow lane. To cut a long legend short, it was one of these nights, about a year into our being in the flat, that the feline made his first and lasting appearance. This was pre-therapy and my cutting had peaked to at least every other night. I was just tidying up the evidence, collecting the tissues and carrying them through to the kitchen bin when I noticed a small black circle on the bean bag just inside Kathryn's bedroom. I assumed it was a discarded jumper; Kathryn is not known for her neatness. But with my next footstep the jumper moved, stretched out a leg and yawned. I looked back and the jumper was now lazily staring in my direction. It stood up, stretched and walked over to me. I knelt down and tickled it under its chin. The jumper purred loudly.

'Well,' I said as the jumper rolled over showing its white tummy, 'I think I just need to go and clear up. Please continue to make yourself at home.'

I wandered into the kitchen and rinsed my wrist. I turned round to see the jumper padding across the kitchen floor where it sat and watched me cleaning the blood from my arm.

'What is your name? I can't keep calling you jumper,' I said, drying my hands as he began to wash his paws, our kitchen floor obviously not clean enough for him.

'How about, erm, Cat? That'll do for now.' After cutting I just didn't have the energy to be any more creative.

He watched me again and waited some more. I gave him some milk and a tin of tuna. He never left.

And here he is again, cradled in Kathryn's arms.

'You're home early,' she says, meaning nothing, but I feel accused.

'Only just got in,' I lie. I blush.

Hide it. Keep it secret. A record of my pain, MY pain.

My head starts again and I wonder why on earth I bothered cutting. She puts Cat down, leaving traces of fur on her black jumper.

'Good day at work?' she asks, getting the milk out of the fridge. 'You were quiet on the email front.'

I didn't go to work.
I got to the bus stop but changed my mind, turned back, went home.
I sat on the floor brewing up a storm in my head.
Look at my arms, look at them, look at what I do to myself.
I hurt, I hurt inside and outside.

'Yeah, I, erm, I, I had meetings most of the day,' I mumble, turning my face, pretending to read the label on the milk carton.

'Oh, tell me about it,' she rolls her eyes in exaggerated annoyance, 'Mike had me taking notes all afternoon whilst...' She carries on, but my mind filters her out.

Back in reality and I try to make sense of why I took the day off work, why I had to cut again. I didn't have to. I was at the bus stop; a bus arrived. I chose not to get on. I chose to go home where I knew I wouldn't be safe. I chose badly.

'...and so I thought I'd invite them round for a meal maybe. What do you think?' She's sitting opposite me, waving a teaspoon around, waiting for my response.

'Yeah, fine, whatever.' I get up and leave the kitchen.

I feel her eyes watching me, her mind ticking over. She knows me too well.

I walk to my bedroom and close the door behind me. I turn to see Cat sitting on my bed waiting for me. Sometimes I swear there are two of him, he was in the kitchen when I left! From that very first meeting when he watched me cleaning up my arm Cat has been a silent conspirator in my cutting activity. Kathryn, even though she is my best friend and flatmate, had no idea about the self-harm when we first moved in together. She knew about my depression – that can be hard to mask – but not the cutting. She knows now of course. I think she has come to expect it and the shock is no longer visible in her eyes when she sees new cuts on my arm. At first I was very vigilant about covering up my arms, not because I didn't trust her but because we were just moving in together and I didn't know how to bring it up:

'Oh yes, I am quite tidy. I like to shower before breakfast and on occasion I take a razor blade to my arm or maybe my left leg depending on my mood.' Plus it is a very private act and until Cat came along it was a lonely thing to do. Cat is allowed to be present on these intimate occasions, simply because he follows me everywhere and would be very put out if I shut the door in his face. To Cat I am a walking milk and meat vending machine, with optional cuddles at no extra cost.

At first it was very surreal, me cutting and Cat washing himself. I would start to feel uncomfortable if he began watching me. But it soon became clear that my need to cut was stronger than the uncomfortable feeling of being watched. In fact Cat became quite considerate, always being present, but seemingly understanding it was an act of solitude, he would never approach me. Like a father watching his daughter swim to the deep end for the first time, far enough away to give her the feeling of achieving by herself, but close enough for her to feel safe. And so it was with Cat. He'd let me stroke him when I otherwise felt inconsolable and he'd let me pay him in tuna and biscuits.

Then one day when I was washing up, Kathryn said to me, 'What did you do to your arm?'

I stopped mid-scrub and studied my arm as if seeing it for the first time.

'Cat,' is all I said.

'Cat? Did that?' she asked, peeling a banana, leaving the peel on the table, as opposed to in the bin.

'Yeah, I should really stop teasing him.'

And in walked Cat, oblivious to the unfounded accusations being made about him. A slur on his good name.

'Cat never hurt anything,' Kathryn laughed but she didn't question my explanation.

Cat sat at my feet looking up at me and I swore he winked, as if to say, 'I won't tell her the truth, as long as you keep filling my bowl up.'

I do believe I am the only person ever to be blackmailed by a cat.

Chapter 7
Let's face the music

Sitting on the bench watching the commuters coming and going I wonder if I'll actually have the courage to ring the doorbell tonight. This is the first time I've been since leaving the drunken phone message two nights ago. Ten to seven. Ten minutes to sit and summon up enough courage to press that buzzer. I like to turn up early and sit and watch the world go by; it seems to settle me. I hate being late and not having the time to sit on my bench and catch my breath. Sometimes when I am late, I still allow myself five minutes to sit here. It's part of my routine and it knocks me off balance if I don't get to do it. I like to watch the people, give them all jobs and guess what their home life is like. Do they wonder why I'm here three times a week? Do they even notice?

The next bunch troops past me and I watch them intently. It's cold and they all wear the commuter's winter uniform. The women have long black coats, with scarves tied snugly around their necks. The men wear beige or grey macs and carry black briefcases and umbrellas, even though it hasn't rained today. I give most of them jobs in the city, accountant, banker and lawyer. Occasionally there are people in jeans and trainers, but still carrying briefcases, trying to hang on to some sort of respectability. These are the IT guys, web designers, systems analysts.

I look at my watch, just gone seven o'clock. I don't want to go in, I don't want to see her face, I'm nervous. What if she shouts at me? What if she hates me? What if she throws me out? I once read that therapists are eternally forgiving. I don't remember where I read it or who wrote it, but I hope they were right. I stand up and walk slowly across the road. The car is parked on the opposite side of the road to number 57, another part of my routine in place. Standing on the doorstep outside the blue front door I take a breath and press the buzzer.

When she opens the door I scan her face for signs of annoyance, or even worse, hatred, but see nothing. She smiles and stands back to let me through, just as usual. The forbidden room has its door shut; I imagine another me sitting with another therapist talking about other worries. The kitchen smells sweet and I spy a bowl full of dried lavender on the worktop. I wonder who needs the calming influence of lavender more, the clients or the therapists! I sit on the couch, but don't put my feet up, I leave them on the floor, one on each side of the couch. My right leg jigs up and down with nerves. She closes the door and sits in her chair behind me. I want her to say something, I want her to break the ice. Don't make me start this conversation. Miraculously she seems to read my mind.

'I got your message and I was unsure if you would come in tonight,' she says, her voice not as soft as usual.

'Yes, I, erm, I'm sorry about the message, I was drunk and I can't actually remember everything I said.' I'm cringing inside, my whole body screwed up into a perfect circle, like a bubble, ready to pop at any moment.

'You said you were in trouble, that you were scared and that you didn't know what to do.' She fills in my memory. 'Do you want to tell me where you were?'

I stay silent, hoping to suddenly float off out of her reach like a bubble. I draw a pattern with my finger on the suede couch and try to form an answer in my mind. I look at the ceiling and realise there is nowhere to float off to. No escape.

'You said you were somewhere you shouldn't be,' she says, probing for an answer. 'Can you say more?'

'I'd had a bit to drink,' I start. 'I went out, for a drink, or two. Then I got on a number three bus,' I say, hoping she'll realise that the number three goes right past the end of her street.

'You're shaking your head,' she says, her voice becoming stern. 'What are you thinking? Did you get on a number three because that's how young you were feeling? Did the child in you want to get out? You sounded like a child on the message, scared and alone.'

I shake my head again. I have my head in my hands now. I have to admit what I did; I can't talk my way round this. She's not going to be happy with any lies, any leaving out the details. She wants to know.

'Did you get off the number three?' her voice a little quieter now, as if she realises she might be scaring me back inside my head too much.

'Yes,' almost a whisper, ' I did. I'm sorry, but I did and I don't know why, but I had to do it, I had to go there, I had to. It is such a strong urge I can't control it.'

'You had to go where?' She's not going to acknowledge she knows. That would be admitting that yes, she does live there, and I know she'll never do that.

I can see no way out so I say the name of her road, the postcode and the house number. She stays silent. 'Where you live,' I say.

She stays silent a long time and I don't think she knows how to deal with this admission from me. I don't think she knows what to say.

Then eventually she asks, 'And why did you go to where you consider me to live? What did you do?'

'I didn't actually do very much,' I say, telling the truth and beginning to feel quite silly. 'I just stood and looked at the

house for a bit, then came to my senses and phoned you.' I
didn't mention the 'Superhero Me' or the cape. That might
just sound too far-fetched.

'Have you done this before?' she asks directly, wanting to
know how often I've stood outside her house.

'Just once,' I admit, as if only once might make it OK.

She sighs, 'You need to learn to bring this in here. You are
not going to find me out there…'

But she's lost me, I'm suddenly somewhere else.

*I'm 15 again, holding a half-empty bottle of martini and sitting in
the front garden of my headmaster's house. It's a cold October night
and I've just heard a church clock strike twice. I shiver, the alcohol
wearing off and leaving me cold. I've been sitting here since 11
o'clock when I watched shadows behind the curtains in an upstairs
window, wondering if it was him. I have no idea. The lights in the
house went off soon after and I think I dozed off, well, passed out
really. I woke up when a cat walked in front of the security light
which shone directly onto my face.*

*Suddenly I'm not sure why I came here; I'm not sure what to do
for the next five hours before the buses start running again. I just
know I had to come here, the urge to be close was too strong to resist.*
I'm alone.
I'm cold.
I'm scared.

This whole thing is a complete repeat of what happened when
I was a teenager. But then I had the excuse of being a teenager,
I could put it down to not knowing any better. I no longer
have that to fall back on, that is no longer the answer. I'm back
in the room, the red curtains unblur into view, and she has
stopped talking. Only the creak of her chair as she rocks back

and forth tells me she is still there. I do something I have never, ever done before; I turn round and look at her.

'Why do I do this?' I say, pleading with her to help me. 'What the hell am I doing?'

I proceed to tell her about the headmaster, about how it got so bad I was nearly expelled, how I knew this would happen again and I should have warned her and that I'm sorry, it won't happen again.

LIAR! WE'RE ALREADY PLANNING YOUR NEXT MOVE. WAIT OUTSIDE AFTER A SESSION, SEE WHO SHE LEAVES WITH, SEE WHICH WAY HER CAR GOES.

I look at her, her face showing no emotion. Then she opens her mouth and I want her to say something to make it better, but she doesn't. She simply says, 'It's time. I'll see you on Wednesday.'

'AAAAAAAAAAAAAGGGGGGGGGGH!' I inwardly scream.

Chapter 8
Treacle Tuesday

Sometimes waiting for a session to come round is so hard. I don't know how it can feel such a long time between Monday and Wednesday but it does. The hours are like treacle, thick and heavy. I have to wade through them, dragging myself forward. No matter how much work I do it's still only ten o'clock on Tuesday morning. Work becomes meaningless; people talk to me but their words make no sense, just a string of noise, thickening the treacle, making my day go more slowly. Work for me is in an office of a charity doing work on the web pages and answering enquiries from staff on how to use certain IT software. Generally it is a very quiet job. I turn up, I switch on my PC, I send a few emails to Kathryn, I leave. The people in the office are all very nice and pleasant, but they're not the most boisterous group I've ever worked with. They get excited if the biscuits have chocolate on them, but nothing else stirs them from their work. Nobody 'does lunch'. At one o'clock I'm often nudged from the edge of a snooze by the rustling of paper bags and the clicking open of lunchboxes as people stay at their desks and eat.

Sometimes the quietness is too much and my mind starts to wander. I long to be busy where I'm always distracted. I stare at my PC, not registering the words on the screen. I just want to be with her, in the room, feeling safe, feeling contained. Sometimes it hurts so much to leave her at the end of a session. It tears me apart to walk past her and I feel the snap as she closes the door on me; something breaks. Sometimes I can barely breathe it hurts so much. I've never told her this. I've never thought it meant anything. I just thought it was me being demanding, being needy, but I'm beginning to think it might be important to talk about, to understand.

I focus on my screen and realise my screensaver has been on for some time. I press the spacebar and see I have three new emails to read. I click onto the first one, but my mind has already wandered. To give myself some breathing space I go and make a cup of tea. I use the wrong end of the spoon to stir it, I use someone else's milk, I drop the tea bag on the floor before managing to get it in the bin. I should be at home in bed. I should be sitting under her desk, curled up, warm and safe by her feet. I sit back down at my PC and notice another email has arrived. It's from Kathryn; I decide to read it. Then somehow, my hand forgets it is holding a cup of tea and just lets go. Tea goes everywhere, but mainly over my keyboard. I swear very loudly in a very quiet office and everyone turns round. If I had said nothing no one would have noticed. I blush and fluster; someone hands me some tissue to mop it up with. I sit back down and watch the brown liquid swirling around at the bottom of my keyboard. I tip it upside down and it trickles onto my desk.

This fiasco however has not stopped my head from working overtime or the others from scurrying away at their work.

How can I possibly understand this feeling? I'm too stuck in the middle of it to see it as anything else but 'I miss her'. And I can't imagine saying all this out loud; how can I possibly describe this feeling in words? There is a wall between my head and my mouth which stops me talking about feelings like this with her. I can sit in the room with her and *think* it all, but the line between brain and mouth has been cut. Then I remember her words from the other day, 'Perhaps you could think about writing it down'. Maybe that's the answer. Only 11 o'clock, it's worth a try; at least it might help me get through Treacle Tuesday a bit faster.

I begin to type a letter to her; at least this makes me look busy. I have no idea how to start so I just start to type what is in my head. It is very exhilarating to be able to get this out of my head and seeing it on the screen will make it less of a muddle for me to understand. Then I notice that either my typing has degenerated since I last did any work or that my keyboard is beginning to stick together with dried-up tea. 'T' sticks when I press it, I have to hit 'e' very hard before it will register and 's' and 'r' don't even work at all. I giggle to myself as I read what I have just typed:

> Each tttime I leave you I find ittt so hard tto nottt wantt to walk ight back in and itt with you again. Ittt hut o badly, ittt like omeone I cuttting my lifeline.

Pen and paper seems to be the most sensible option as I wait for my keyboard to dry out and recover. I write for some time and I'm hardly aware of what is hurtling from my mind to the end of the pen, but it feels good. It's almost like talking to her. Then I notice some of the words that I have been using, 'want', 'need', 'love' and I put my pen down to read it back for the first time:

> I don't know where to start. I'm trying to write things down for you, trying to get them to make sense for both of us I guess.
>
> I don't mean any harm when I go looking for you; I'm not even sure I want to find you, but the urge is so strong, it's as if I have to fill this need

with something and at the moment this need is you.

When you shut the door on me I feel a snap, like someone cutting my lifeline. Pure panic hits me and for a moment I don't know how I am going to survive without you. It's almost like love. I know that's silly, but that's how it feels. If I don't see you my heart will break and everything will tumble around my ears. I need you there to keep me safe. Without you I feel as if I'll fall into the void. I want you so badly but I know this can't be real, I just need you to help me understand this. I'm sorry I annoyed you. I will try to control it.

I sit back in my chair and take deep breaths. Did I just write that? It makes me sound like a freak, but it's exactly how it feels. I re-read it, scribbling out the last line, as I'm not sure I can keep this promise. I fold the letter up and put it under my keyboard, which looks as though it might have dried out.

This is my fourth job since graduating. I get bored very easily. I'm still not sure what I want to do in life. I've found when applying for jobs that they sound much more exciting on paper than they actually are in real life. This one sounded quite hi-tech and energetic on paper. In real life I get to email friends an awful lot, so much so that if I'm in a meeting for an hour I go back to my inbox to find people complaining about my absence or wondering if I have gone home sick. I honestly think I could do my work in half the time they employ me for, but I like the money, so I sit and type emails, looking busy. I see my boss making a beeline for my desk, so I switch from the game of solitaire to a spreadsheet of internet usage statistics.

'I have you down for your appraisal this afternoon at two o'clock,' she says, flicking noisily through her diary, most of which seems boringly blank. 'Is that still OK? You're not too snowed under, are you?'

I look at my neat desk and refrain from saying that even if I was snowed under I would still have time to make a snowman. And his family. And three cats and a snow hamster. 'Yes, that's fine, Julie.' I click quietly onto my online diary, 'I've got room G34 and it is no probs.'

She smiles, loudly snaps her diary closed and walks off towards another unsuspecting solitaire player. I click quietly from my online diary to my game of solitaire. My boss knows about my therapy. When I first started here I had to ask for flexi-time to leave early on a Monday and a Wednesday. She was fine about it and quickly told me she had worked with someone with depression before and coped very well. I congratulated her on her ability to deal with depression second-hand. OK, I didn't, but only because she was trying her hardest not to be patronising. She meant well, as most people do. It was just the look in her eyes when I mentioned 'therapy' that gave away what her mind was really thinking, and it went something like this:

'Oh my God, I've employed a fruit loop.'

I think she expected me to be having breakdowns at regular intervals and to be in tears most of the day, but of course it is not like that and it is only mentioned in situations such as appraisals.

So two o'clock finally dawdled round, after what seemed like about three weeks and an endless hour of listening to my silent colleagues trying to eat food quietly. I watched Barbara subtly from behind my newspaper and I could see her licking all the flavour off her crisps and then sucking them till they were soft enough to chew without making the normal crisp sort of sound. I wondered if it was time to find another job.

I got to room G34 at the same time as my boss was unlocking the door and we did the embarrassing jostle of who would go through the door first. She won and grabbed the only chair not in full sun, so I spent the next 40 minutes squinting at her and seeing only her silhouette. She flicked noisily through her diary then through a pad of lined paper, sharpened her pencil and wrote the date on the top line.

'So, appraisal,' she said and wrote something else on the next line. 'What we'll do is I'll start and tell you things from my perspective then we'll swap over and you get a go.'

I lost the will to live there and then. My brain slid out of my ears and went skipping away with the fairies. I was left with only the capacity to nod and 'hmm' in all the right places. My brain, along with the fairies, started dressing the silhouette in silly hats and moustaches, large plastic noses and thick-rimmed glasses. I of course could only 'hmm' and nod whilst my mind rolled on the floor, thumping its fists with joy and weeping with laughter. It was the best time it had had in ages so I didn't even try to stop it as it took her pencil and poked it into her right ear. At this point she was starting to talk about how my therapy was fitting in with work and it was difficult to take her seriously in a pink bowler hat, with a ginger handlebar moustache and a pencil sticking out of one ear.

I told her it was 'fine', as I tell anybody who doesn't really know me, because let's face it, she doesn't really want to know that actually I'm having a really hard time keeping things together and I'd quite like a few weeks off just to hide under my duvet. No, most people just like to hear you say, 'it's fine.'

Chapter 9
Bedrooms and nests

I survived the appraisal and Wednesday finally appeared. I seem to sit all day staring at the clock on my PC watching it tick from nine o'clock all the way to half four, when I get up and walk out of the office. The most exciting part of the day is when Phil nearly chokes to death on a mini-cheddar. I watch him struggling not to cough really loudly for a whole ten minutes before he gets up, very red-faced and goes into the corridor where we can all hear him trying to dislodge the rogue cheesy biscuit.

The letter I wrote yesterday is neatly typed and folded up in my coat pocket. I have not decided whether I will let her read it. I don't know whether I can trust her with my feelings. I couldn't bear it if she trampled on my feelings. In a childish way this part of me that is scared has stormed off and in a melodramatic flourish has slammed its imaginary bedroom door on the rest of me. Consequently I'm feeling quite cheerful as at 4.40pm I sit on the upstairs deck of a bus travelling to therapy.

The bus stops outside a busy shopping centre and what feels like half the population of North London ascends up the stairs to keep me company. A harassed-looking man with a baby and too many bags of shopping sits in front of me. The baby is draped over his shoulder and stares at me with small green eyes. I smile and look out of the window trying to ignore it. It's not that I don't like babies, my brother has three.

They're great from a distance, but not drooling over the edge of the seat onto my shoes. The man finally notices and turns his child around, smiling sheepishly at me.

The clouds look heavy and I know it will be raining by the time I have to get off the bus, and I have no umbrella. That means my hair will get wet and go flat and I'll turn up at therapy looking as if I've been swimming in the Thames for a week. I smile, and tell myself it doesn't matter what I look like; I don't have to impress her, and I'm not there to impress her. I hear the imaginary bedroom door being slammed again.

Inside the imaginary bedroom I sit on a bed, legs pulled up to my chest, eyebrows furrowed and a black cloud hovering above my head. The walls of the bedroom are covered with writing, words strung together that don't make sense, written in the hand of a child. A child trying to make meaning of the world, shut away from everyone else. A lonely child. A scared child.

Arms folded I sit there and stare at the door I have just slammed. I'm sulking. I'm sulking because I can't have my own way. Sulking because things are happening and I don't understand them – I'm too young to understand them. I'm sulking because the adults are talking about things and leaving me out. They're too busy to talk to me; I'm too small for them to notice. I don't know what to do so I'll just sit here and be quiet, keeping my emotions in my head. I don't want to worry them, they look awfully busy. I'm a good girl.

The clouds see me get off the bus and let the rain fall as heavily as they can, big drops bouncing off the pavement, running down the gutters. I pull up the collar on my coat, as if this will stop the rain from hitting me and hurry towards my destination.

I'm actually early, but my bench has no shelter and is soaking already, so I continue walking straight past and up the road. I walk past the car and stop to take a peek inside. A CD lies on the passenger seat; I don't recognise the face on the cover, but a mental image of it has been burned into memory should I ever see it in a shop. There is a red umbrella on the back seat along with a jacket and a London A–Z. I realise I probably appear very suspicious should anyone be watching me and continue walking along the road. All the leaves have fallen from the trees now, but no one has been to sweep them up, and with the rain the leaves are soggy and as slippy as ice to walk on. I carry on round the corner trying not to fall, holding on to trees and fences as I go. The road takes me in a big loop back to my bench. It's still raining, but it's time for my session. I walk up the path, the security light beams on and I press the buzzer.

After being out in the cold and the rain the therapy room is almost too warm, or maybe it's that I'm blushing as she reads the letter I handed her as I arrived. I cringe as I try to guess which bit she's got to. Has she hit upon the word 'need' yet, is she trying not to laugh at the word 'love'? I close my eyes and listen as she 'ummms' and 'hmmms' at various places.

I hear the letter being placed on the desk and she leans back in her chair. I'm very small now, hoping to fall in between the creases of material on the couch, hoping she's not going to laugh at me, hoping she doesn't run out of the room waving the letter in the air, fits of laughter escaping from her as she barges in to the other therapy room to show how stupid and childish one of her clients is.

'I see you've been having a difficult time containing yourself since the last session,' she says. I sense no concealed laughter in her voice. 'I think you were very brave to write this letter; it's very well written.'

I run my hands through my hair and clasp my fingers together behind my head. My elbows by the side of my head hide my face from her, hide my relief.

'I wrote it at work, in one go,' I explain. 'It says what I'd like to say in here, but can never quite get my mouth to hook up with my thoughts.'

Silence.

'Talk to me, carry on where the letter left off,' she nudges, but she's pushed just that bit too hard and suddenly I've fallen down one of the creases in the sofa and am making a nest out of bits of fluff. When I was little I used to hide under my bed and hope my mum wouldn't know where I was so I didn't have to go to Sunday School. I feel that same feeling now.

I peel back the crease and shout, 'I need to understand what is going on. I need to be able to justify this to my sane self.' Through the bedroom door I can hear things being thrown at the walls. I'm getting impatient. 'The two parts of me don't understand each other, I just need something to bridge that gap.'

I'm confused and angry and want to climb out of my crease and put my foot through the windows that I know are behind the red curtains. I'd like to rip those curtains down and smash the glass with my bare fist. I want to scream out loud, but I don't; it has to stay on the inside. Let it thrash about as much as it wants, on the inside, in the bedroom.

'It must be very hard for you,' her voice is quiet and calming. 'I know how hard it is for you at the end of a session; I know you find the separation very difficult.'

'Tell me what you mean,' I say, forgetting about my nest and coming back into the room.

'I think with you there are two elements going on.' She settles in for a long therapist explanation. 'On the one hand you need to be close to me and at the end of each session, when I shut the door on you, you see that as me turning you away. There is always something you have to hide, always part of you that you hide.'

But her voice has soothed me away and I have found where my head went.

I'm seven years old.
We're at the hospital visiting my dad.
He's had another heart attack.
I heard the ambulance men take him away during the night.
He's in intensive care. Children aren't allowed.
It's my brother's eleventh birthday. He can go in and see him.
I'm standing at the doorway watching.
Alone.
My dad beckons me in and I scuttle towards his bed.
I lean over to hug him, but he tells me to go round the other side because all the wires in his arm get in the way.
'Be careful now,' I hear a voice say, 'Don't get too close.'

My head is spinning. Sometimes things make sense but as soon as they do, they're gone and I'm left feeling dizzy. I rub my eyes and take a deep breath, ready to talk to her, but:
'It's time.'

Chapter 10
Well trained

I walk out of the session still feeling dazed. I feel the door shut behind me and want to burst into tears. I sit on the wet bench, very still, trying to stop the spinning. Sometimes it is hard going back to childhood and feeling things that you were too young to feel back then. I never knew I was scared, or alone, not until now. I can feel the rain on the bench soaking through my jeans. I stand up and lean against a wall, trying to think of nice things. All I can think about are pink bowler hats and ginger moustaches, but for now at least it makes me smile.

The string of commuters coming off the trains is getting shorter and sparser; these late arrivals look more harassed than their earlier counterparts. After ten minutes or so I see someone else approaching the front door of number 57 and pressing the buzzer. I wonder if it is her next client. I watch the person enter and imagine her opening the door on some-one else, not me. Has she forgotten about me already? I want to go and press the buzzer and interrupt them, make her think about me, but I know I mustn't. I stand up and walk away. I feel my heart stretching from the doorway of number 57, getting thinner and thinner. As I cross over the railway bridge it gets to breaking point and snaps as loudly as my boss closing her diary.

I stop and peer over the wall at the train tracks below. The wall is high and I have to stand on my tiptoes to see over, making me feel like a small child. I'd like to be sitting on top of the wall, swinging my legs back and forth, watching the little trains stop at the platform whilst the big trains whistle past, too important for such a small station.

The next thing I know I'm scrabbling up the wall, my feet and knees scraping against the brick, as my arms strain to pull me up. I swing one leg over the top of the wall and lie there a minute as I get my balance. I sit up and feel the wind in my face. I'm level with the top of the trees up here and I can see some birds' nests still clinging to the branches, empty and derelict. Looking out, up the railway track, fog swirls about, as if everyone in North London has breathed out at once, their breath visible and merging in the cold air.

I see the lights of a train approaching. It's coming fast, a big one. Its horn sounds as it rushes beneath the bridge, sending cold air spiralling around me, making the trees dance momentarily. I remember sitting on a hill at the side of a railway track with my dad when I was younger. He would get me to write down the numbers of the trains as he shouted them to me. I could barely hear him from beneath the sound of the engines roaring past. Those were great days, just me, my dad and a pile of cold sausage sandwiches. My brother never used to come with us; he thought it was sissy to sit and watch trains. That never bothered me. I wasn't there because of the trains, I was there because of my dad. Another train whizzes past me and I can feel the bridge vibrate under the sound. The windows flash by too fast to see any passengers, but it makes you want to wave all the same. It makes me want to turn to my dad and ask him where the train is going and where will it stop, because he would know. He knows everything, my dad. I sit and feel like a child again.

Then too quickly my watch says it is time for her last client to be leaving. I swing my leg back over the wall and slither down to the ground. I walk back up towards my bench and sit there.

WAITING.
LIKE CAT. JUST WAITING.

The light in the hallway of number 57 is switched on and moments later the front door opens and the person I saw pressing the buzzer 50 minutes ago walks out, turning left and walking up the road away from me and my bench. I keep my eye on the door of number 57. I can hear a dim voice trying to shout from somewhere way back in my head that I should be going home now. But it is easy to ignore. The sound of the trains still in my mind drowns out any sensible voices. I get off my bench and stand in the doorway of a nearby takeaway shop.

WAITING.

The light comes on again in the hallway of number 57. The front door opens and she walks out, zipping up a black jacket and pulling on her gloves. The car is parked up the road. She doesn't even look in my direction; she doesn't even know I'm there. I watch her get into the car and pull the seatbelt across. She turns the key and the engine starts up, the lights are switched on and she's signalling to pull out. I step out of the doorway, into the light of a lamp post, and watch as she drives past. I don't know if she sees me, but I want to follow her, I don't want her out of my sight. I want to scream.

Don't go!
Don't leave me!
Let me go with you!
I don't want to be on my own!

I think I'm going to faint. I sit down on the bench and put my head in my hands. I shake my head and wonder why I do this to myself. I have a warm flat, a fat cat and flatmate cooking at home. I should be there. I laugh out loud at the thought of Kathryn actually cooking something, but the image is enough to tear me away from the bench and the cold streets of North London.

I get home to the smell of cooking onions and garlic and wonder if I have walked into the wrong flat.

'Hey, you!' Kathryn greets me from the kitchen. I walk in to find her clad in an apron and armed with a wooden spoon.

I sit at the kitchen table and feign speechlessness. She giggles.

'Remember that guy I met the other week?' she asks. I don't, but I nod anyway. 'Well, I invited him for a meal next Friday, so I thought perhaps I should learn to cook. In other words you're being my guinea pig.' She adds some sliced tomato to the onions and garlic. 'How was therapy?' she asks, as she always does. We both know I might not give a full answer, but she likes me to know the option to talk is always there should I need to.

'Yeah, so so,' I say neutrally, picking up onion peel from the floor and depositing it in the bin.

'Your mum phoned, by the way,' Kathryn says, adding perhaps too much dried thyme to the sauce.

'Oh yeah, did she say what she wanted?' I ask, wiping tomato seeds up from the floor.

'She's your mother; she wanted to say hello to her youngest offspring; she doesn't need another excuse,' Kathryn retorted, tasting the sauce, turning up her nose and adding more thyme.

'Maybe I'll ring her tomorrow,' I reply, setting the table for an unexpected dinner.

To my amazement Kathryn cooked a full three-course meal that was not only edible but made me realise that from now on she could do this every week! I went to bed with not only a full mind from therapy but a very full belly.

Chapter 11
Dream on

The room I'm sitting in is therapy but at the same time it isn't.

The furniture has changed and isn't in the same place. The window looks out onto fields. We're one floor up and the sun is shining. I'm on a large couch that might be a bed but I can't quite tell. There are lots of throws and cushions and it is terribly comfortable. I feel very relaxed. I turn my head and watch you writing something down on a pad of paper. You look at me and smile. Outside in the field lambs play and chase each other, whilst birds swoop and sing in the blue sky.

You're talking on the telephone but I'm not sure what you're saying. I'm just listening to the tone of your voice and the lilt of your accent. It doesn't matter what you're saying, I just want to swim in the colours of your voice. There is a man standing in the corner of the room. I can't see his face, he is all in shadow, but I am not disturbed by his presence. I keep watching you out of the corner of my eye.

You come and sit next to me; there are suddenly piles of pictures of me as a child on the bed, and I'm trying to stop them from falling to the floor as you pull a throw over our legs. There are pictures of me on swings, standing next to flowering bushes and kneeling on the beach. In all of them I am on my own.

I can feel the heat of your body next to me. Then you place one hand on my leg and squeeze gently. My whole body is filled with a warm glow and I'm intensely happy and safe, so, so safe and content.

The feeling in the dream is so strong it wakes me and I am utterly disappointed that it wasn't real, that it isn't real. I close my eyes and keep hold of the feeling, the feeling that you wanted me, that you were there for me, that...my alarm clock sounds.

Chapter 12
Timber!

I sit and fidget with the corner of my shirt, pulling at a loose piece of thread. My head has been floating all day since the dream, getting higher and higher, until it was drenched in a pool of bliss. I want to turn round and ask her to talk to me as she did last night. I want to go and kneel beside her chair and just watch her doing whatever it is that psychotherapists do. I want to curl up on her lap and snuggle into her belly, mingle with her body and drift around in her mind.

She's watching me. I hide the smile, the warm glow in my stomach.

'So,' she says, creaking in the chair as she gets comfortable, 'how are you today?'

'I'm good,' I say, the smiling breaking out on my face.

'You seem happy.'

I pull the thread of my shirt. 'Yeah, I feel high today.' The image of her squeezing my leg rushes headlong into my mind, like a high-speed train. I feel it hit the front of my head and dance about. I'm surprised she can't see it.

'Do you want to tell me why?' I hear the suspicion rise in her voice.

'I had a dream last night,' I say. 'It was so real. You know the kind of dream where you can still feel the atmosphere when you wake?'

'Mmmmm?' Her cue for me to carry on talking.

My head is still floating, spiralling above me, like a bird in flight.

'It was about you and me. It was set in therapy but it wasn't here. It was different.'

I can hear the scratch of her pen on the paper. She likes it when I tell her about dreams, a peep into my unconscious. I tell her about the furniture being different, about there being a bed, about the view of fields. I mention her on the phone, the photos of me as a child. I stop. I can't possibly tell her about the leg touching; even though it was only a dream, my head has made it real. Then I remember about the man in the shadows. 'I don't know who he was, but it felt right that he was there. It was about his just being there, in the background. Does that make sense?'

'Yes,' she says, 'yes, it does. It sounds like your father, like the way he was always there, but very silent. But the presence of him makes you feel comfortable and safe.'

'Yes, that's right,' I nod, ' but there was more to the dream than that. He didn't figure in the feeling of the dream. He was just there really.'

She doesn't respond. She knows there is more. I sit still for a while, wondering how to word it, how to tell her that she touched me. Should she not already know? Is she not aware of what she did? Of course not, it was a dream, a dream, a dream. It wasn't real. I almost giggle out loud.

'You came to sit next to me,' I continue, 'and you got under the duvet and you...you...you put your hand on my leg.' My stomach flips, 'And I just felt so safe, so content. And I can still feel that now.'

I stop. Close my eyes. Waiting for her reaction.

'Tell me more about the photos.' She avoids what I thought was the most important part of the dream. I oblige and describe them the best I can remember, that they were of me, as a child, alone.

'Tell me what you felt about the photos; why were you trying to stop them falling off?'

I can't remember. I just remember feeling complete bliss; there was no other feeling.

'I do think there were other feelings,' she says, quite bluntly, 'but you chose only to focus on the one that felt safe, the one that wasn't uncomfortable. You were able to ignore everything else apart from the one feeling you know leaves you high. It is almost as if you throw yourself into me then you don't have to deal with anything else. The photos sound awfully lonely, like a reminder of how you felt as a child, yet you had no feeling about it? I think the man in the shadow and the photos are connected, but you just pushed yourself into this blissful feeling, hiding from what is real.'

She stops. Having kicked the air out of my sails she watches me hurtle back down, landing with a crash. A petal falls off one of the flowers as if knocked loose by the shudder of my landing. I feel my eyes fill with tears. I'm shell-shocked. She's just let me fall so far and didn't even try to catch me. I sit there for a while, grabbing tightly to the edge of the couch, blinking back the tears. I'm not sure if they are tears of anger or of fright.

'I can't believe you just did that,' I say through clenched teeth. 'I can't believe you just let me fall like that. I just came crashing down.'

I wipe my eyes, still reeling from the shock of falling so far, sitting very still so I don't fall any further. I want to turn round and grab her by the collar of her shirt, bring her face close to mine. Scare her as she just scared me.

'I couldn't have you getting so high that you flew off out of reach,' she explains. 'I needed to reel you back in.'

'But you didn't have to do it so abruptly,' I argue.

'Yes, I did. If I let you get any higher you might never come down. You needed to know why you were there, that by clinging onto me you are avoiding the real feelings. Your high was not real.'

She kicks me a little bit further down. I'm left wondering why she doesn't stand on me and squash me flat altogether.

'It's time.'

I hate her. I hate that she is leaving me like this. I don't look at her. I walk straight past and never want to go back. I slam the front door behind me and stand there, catching my breath, fighting back the tears. But there are too many to fight back and I start to cry. I want to run away as fast as I can and never come back. I want to bang on the door for her to come and rescue me. I want to sit on the doorstep and wait for the rain to wash me away. I don't know what I want. I walked in there on top of the world; now I feel as if I'm underground with no way out. I turn and run. I run until my lungs hurt, until my knees begin to buckle. But no matter how hard and fast I run, I can't escape myself.

Chapter 13

Anthropomorphic adventures

I begin to feel much better after my impromptu running session and wonder if I shouldn't make it more of a regular occurrence and not just when a therapy session goes badly. I get home, hang up my coat and phone my mum before I forget. We talk on the phone quite a lot, but I sometimes feel guilty because it is her who always phones me and she often phones when I'm out at therapy. She doesn't know, you see, about therapy. I've never quite worked out a way of how to tell her. I'm not sure she'd understand. She's from the background of not moaning about stuff, just getting on and doing. And I think she'd worry. She'd not understand what therapy is and she'd think I was on the verge of suicide or something and start asking too many questions and need to know what she did wrong that I'm so unhappy. It's easier if she doesn't know. I dial her number but there is no answer. Maybe I'll try again tomorrow.

The next morning I stretch, yawn and kick the cat off my bed, who has probably been asleep there most of the night. Surely it is too early to get up for work. Even with the curtains drawn I can tell it is still very dark outside and there is the faint drumming of rain on the window. I make a split-second decision not to go to work – it is way too horrible outside – so I turn over and scrunch my eyes up, trying to magic myself asleep, trying to ignore the nagging feeling left over from yesterday's therapy session. I still can't believe she whipped my safety net away.

I toss and turn, can't get comfortable. Cat sits on the other pillow next to me, whining for his breakfast. I hear Kathryn padding about in bare feet making breakfast, getting ready to go to work.

'Go and ask Kathryn – she's in the kitchen already – you dumb animal,' and I push him gently off onto the carpet. He lands with a thud and the bedroom door opens a little as he lets himself out.

Kathryn switches the radio on and I pull the duvet over my head, determined to get back to sleep, chase dreams.

The slamming of the front door as Kathryn leaves for work wakes me. It seems awfully dark until I realise the duvet is still covering my head. I swing my legs over the side of the bed and drag myself into a standing position. I begin to wonder whether if I stand here long enough Cat will bring me a cup of strong coffee and maybe some toast. On cue, he walks into the bedroom, sits down and proceeds to wash behind his ears.

'I guess that answers my question then, eh, fat boy?' I say to him. He ignores me.

The kitchen floor is cold on my bare feet. Through the open blind I see that it has stopped raining and is actually beginning to look quite bright. I start to wonder what to do with myself today. I flick the switch on the kettle and take the least dirty cup from the table, swill it out with hot water and spoon a heap of coffee into it. Opening the fridge for the milk I see a bottle of cider, left over from the last dinner party we had, sitting lonely and unloved on the top shelf. I can feel an idea forming.

THIS IS GREAT!
WHY HAVEN'T WE THOUGHT OF THIS BEFORE?
SHE'LL HAVE TO TAKE CARE OF US NOW.

I'm not so sure. This could easily backfire, but what the hell, I have nothing else planned this afternoon.

I pick up the phone and dial her number. After three rings the answerphone clicks on and I leave a message. I ask her if I can come and see her today. I've not gone to work and am scared of what I will do. I hang up, shake my head as if I am ashamed of myself and sit down to drink my coffee.

The rest of the morning passes without incident. I leave a message at work, trying to sound suitably ill and sit watching rubbish TV. I eat some lunch and crack open the bottle of cider. It is sweet and cold, but goes down well. It was a special organic cider and stronger than I am used to, perhaps a little too strong but never mind.

The phone rings. I stand and look at it. I can sense who it is.

'Hello?' I say, my voice croaking.

'Hello,' she replies and says who she is as if introducing herself for the first time. She offers me a slot at five o'clock; I snap it up greedily, hoping my voice doesn't sound too slurred. She tells me to stay calm, to stay at home and that she will see me later. But I know I'm not staying at home. My plan doesn't include staying at home.

My head is spinning a little as I try to tie the laces on my trainers. I manage eventually, with a little help from Cat, who seems intent on trying to catch the end of the lace every time I try to make a bow. I pull my fleece on and empty the contents of my bus pass wallet onto the table. At the last shake the blade falls out with a clatter. It looks a bit past its best; rust has started to form round one edge, so I go to the bathroom, to the airing cupboard and retrieve a hidden blade from under one of the shelves. I repack my wallet, adding the new blade and set off out. The sun is very bright and low in the sky making me squint. I am the only one waiting at the bus stop which makes me think I might have just missed one, but then round the corner appears another. Despite it being only early afternoon the bus is busy and I stand downstairs, squashed between two giggling schoolgirls, obviously over-excited at skipping classes. I put my earphones in and turn the music up, drowning out the inane chatter of the two teenagers. I must reek of alcohol because as soon as there is space people move away from me, always wary of a drunk person in the middle of the day.

I idly gaze out of the bus window watching the different types of shops going by. There are Turkish wedding shops, Greek bakers and Jewish accountants. There are two florists side by side each with suspiciously coloured flowers, as if in competition for the world's most garish bloom. The number of doors in London never ceases to amaze me. The bus passes six doors within a few metres of each other, all supposedly leading to bars and clubs. Either they are very small bars and clubs or London is just one big Tardis! The size of London makes me feel insignificant, invisible. I like that. I like to be anonymous, where no one cares what I'm doing, where no one asks me why I'm drunk in the middle of the day.

The bus pulls up outside a big shopping centre and the driver announces, 'Last stop'. It is my stop anyway but most other passengers make a fuss and raise their eyebrows and complain to the person next to them that they thought it was going on further and now they will have to wait for another and lose their seat. I leave them fuming at the bus stop and walk round the corner to catch the next bus to my destination, Alexandra Palace.

It's a great view from up here, sitting on a grassy bank looking out over London. Over to the left I can see the tall buildings of the city near where I should be at work. I see a train heading towards Kings Cross and can work out where the railway bridge I sat on is, but trees and buildings hide it. My head is still swimming from the cider. It is nearly four o'clock. Bus rides in London always take longer than I expect.

I only have half an hour until I need to start making my way to therapy.

I take out my bus pass and retrieve the blade, holding it carefully in my palm, as if it is the most precious thing I own. Suddenly a big, black dog lollops out from behind some bushes and rushes past me, sniffing every tree, examining every fallen twig. I close my hand into a fist around the blade as his owner walks round the corner, whistling a tune. He nods a hello. I smile back. I watch man and dog disappear down the path and unfurl my fist. It is windy up here and I wish I'd worn a scarf and gloves. The sun is beginning to set already and it will only get colder. I push the sleeve of my jacket up to my elbow and look at the scars on my arm.

This one is for you.
This is how much I hurt.

I'm jolted back to the real world by the reappearance of the big, black dog. He sits in front of me and stares at the blade in my hand. His presence makes me feel guilty. I can imagine what he is thinking and suddenly in my head I hear him say, 'What are you doing with that?' in a deep, echoing, very posh accent. He leans forward and nudges my hand clasping the blade with his nose. 'You're not going to do what I think you're going to do, are you?' he bellows at me, sniffing the scars on my arm.

'What the hell was in that cider?' I chuckle. 'Anyway, I'll do what I want. Thanks for your concern.' I look around again for the owner, hoping he'll come and retrieve his over-concerned pet.

The big, black dog puts a paw on my knee. I put my hand on his paw. I realise it is my own mind asking me these questions and that the dog is just very friendly. I ruffle his head and ask, 'So what's your name?'

'General Reginald Parker the Second,' I imagine him barking, still nosing the blade in my hand, 'and I'm here to remind you that this too will pass.'

'I'm sorry?' I say, still not quite sure why my mind is pretending to be a dog. 'You're here to do what?'

He stands up, and parades up and down in front of me. 'This too shall pass. This feeling, whatever it might be, will pass. My army motto, don't you know,' he says.

I hear his owner shouting to him from down the hill.

'Reggie! Come on, boy!'

I laugh, 'You're really called Reginald?' But the dog is over by the bin, sniffing in some old newspaper. His ears prick up at his owner's voice and he bounds off down the hill, but I'm sure he turns round and salutes before he goes over the top.

'This too shall pass,' I say quietly, breathing deeply. I repeat it gently, beginning to understand the meaning, but I've already gone too far and still need to cut despite General Reginald Parker the Second and his helpful motto.

Within five minutes I'm licking my finger and rubbing at my arm, cleaning up some of the blood. My stomach is still warm from the cider and my head is calmer now. It must be nearly time to set off to therapy; the lights of the city are being switched on as dusk settles over London.

Chapter 14
Ejected

There are five teenagers hanging round my bench when I arrive, so I hover around on the opposite side of the road. The group eye me up suspiciously and I turn away, glancing at my watch as if I am waiting to meet someone. I look round and the group have pulled their hoods up and are sauntering down the road, heading towards an Indian takeaway. I take my chance and go to sit on my bench. Five minutes. Perfect timing. I feel quite clear-headed, but can now feel the organic cider sloshing nauseatingly round my stomach. I really need to pee, but there is nowhere I can go, so I do my best to ignore it.

I stand at the same door I slammed yesterday evening and I can feel my anger with her welling up inside. I press the buzzer and wait for her voice. It sometimes takes her a while to answer the door and I have all sorts of theories as to what she is doing in there, but mainly the notion that she is tidying away evidence of her life outside that office. I imagine her closing notebooks, filing letters, turning off her laptop, switching off her mobile, becoming the therapist, nothing more, nothing less. Eventually she answers and I get let in. I smile meekly as I pass her, feeling as if I'm intruding on her time, aware that she didn't have to see me at all if she didn't want to. She could have pretended she was fully booked; I would never have known.

I sit on my hands and hang my head feeling like a naughty child, and also feeling light-headed from the alcohol and from coming out of the cold into a warm room. She sits behind me and waits for me to begin.

'Thank you for seeing me today,' I say, my eyes on the floor. 'I'm sorry if it's messing you about at all.'

I'm sure I hear her sigh. 'That's fine, I offered you the time, so it is not messing me about. I'm glad you felt you could call.'

The ever-forgiving therapist. 'Do you want to tell me why you didn't go to work?' she asks.

'After last night's session I felt awful. It is the first time I've just wanted to run away from here. I felt let down by you and I guess I had to come today to make myself feel better.'

'To see that I'm still here? To see that I can take you?'

My head mulls over the questions. 'Yes, I suppose so,' I say, editing out the part about the cutting and wanting her to take care of me.

We both fall silent. I used to hate the silences. I'd get all embarrassed and feel I had to fill them with irrelevant chatter. But now I can sit here and not speak; sometimes I like to see who can go longest without speaking. I've found I usually win, because she can't stand not knowing what is going on in my head.

'Is there anything you want to tell me?' she says cryptically.

'Like what?' I ask stubbornly.

'Have you done anything you shouldn't have?'

My mind flicks about doing somersaults. I suddenly feel guilty, but for no reason. I haven't been to her house since the phone call. OK, I've wanted to but that's nothing she needs to know, is it?

'Erm, I don't think so,' I say, hesitantly.

I hear her sigh; this time it was an unmistakeable sigh. I stay silent.

She rubs her hands over her face and her voice starts off muffled as she asks, 'Have you been drinking?' I blush. In my head a door bursts open and six cheerleaders can-can their way into the room.

'Give us a D! Give us an R! Give us an I! Give us an N! Give us a K! and what have you got?' They shout and shake their pom-poms about furiously, 'DRRRRRINK!' They cartwheel out of the room and close the door quietly behind them.

I giggle, unable to keep the image from my mind.

'It must have been strong because you reek of alcohol.'

'I'm sorry,' I whisper. 'I didn't mean to annoy you.'

'Don't be sorry, it's your decision whether you want to drink or not. I'm annoyed at the fact you made me ask you.'

'I didn't want to say. I knew you wouldn't approve.' I fold my arms in defiance.

I feel the sting of the new cut on my arm, but no, I won't tell her about this now. I can tell she's already angry at me and I won't get what I wanted. She won't want to take care of me, she'll just want to analyse it, ask me why I had to do it. I stare daggers into the curtains.

After what I estimate to be at least five minutes of silence from me and more agitated sighs from her, she speaks. 'If you're drunk I don't think there is much point you being here.'

I rip the curtains up with my mind, roll them into a little ball, set fire to them and swallow them, feeling the heat rise up from my stomach, into my cheeks. Anger.

'I might as well go then,' and I lean forward to pick up my coat, expecting her to stop me. 'If you want to throw me out, fine.'

'I don't want to throw you out,' she says quickly, 'You have given me no choice. I don't work with people who have been drinking. It is not me who is throwing you out, it is you who has been drinking. But I do think we should leave it there for today.'

WELL, THAT WENT REALLY WELL, DIDN'T IT?
WELL DONE. VERY EFFECTIVE, OF COURSE SHE'LL WANT TO
TAKE CARE OF US...

'Shut up!' It isn't until I see her looking at me that I realise I
said it out loud. 'Oh, not you, I, I, erm...'

'That's fine. Just come back tomorrow when we can talk
about it properly, yes?' Her voice is softer now.

'Yes, OK.' I drag my coat behind me as she shows me to
the door. I feel very small, very silly, and I can feel the anger
swelling up inside. I watch her back as she walks to the door. I
suddenly want to surge forward, slam her face into the wall. I
hate her for not playing my games, I hate her for knowing me
so well and I hate her for making me leave when it should be
so obvious I need her. She turns round. I lower my eyes in case
they show what I have just been thinking.

'You'll go straight home?' she asks as I pass her at the door.

'Maybe,' I say. This is not the right answer I know, but
right now I don't think she deserves the right answer.

Then as soon as I hear the click of the door shutting behind
me I want to scream out loud, 'I'm sorry. I'm sorry I'm such a
stupid, childish shit, but I don't know what else to do and you
won't help me.' But of course I don't scream, I say it very
quietly, tears falling down my cheeks. I turn round, feeling
quite helpless. I suddenly feel unreal, as if my body is dis-
integrating, I can no longer tell where air starts and my body
ends. I sit down heavily on the steps that lead to the upstairs
flats. I wonder what I look like to her. Childish? Vulnerable?
Insecure? Or just a stubborn drunk?

I cheer myself up with the image of the cheerleaders and
start to repeat General Reginald Parker the Second's motto in
my head: 'This too shall pass, this too shall pass.' With that I
stand up, take a deep breath and go home, where I can cause
no one any damage, or myself any more embarrassment.

I forget to phone my mum.

Chapter 15
An understanding

I wake up the next day with a hangover. For some reason my head had told me it would be a good idea to buy some more cider at the corner shop. I vow never to buy drink based on anger after a session again. Kathryn did warn me. She said that only teenagers and people on park benches drank that sort of cider. I'd laughed and said that I have earned enough bench time, since starting therapy, to become an honorary Cheap Cider Drinker; all I needed was the fingerless gloves. She'd tutted in a motherly way and left me to it, choosing to go to a yoga class rather than sit and watch her flatmate wallow in self-pity.

She found me on the bathroom floor when she got back. Apparently I had covered myself in a towel and was using a dressing gown as a pillow. I don't remember any of this and have asked to see hard evidence before I admit that I sank so low! She said she had then half carried and half dragged me to bed, leaving the empty cider bottle on the pillow next to me to remind me of my binge as soon as I awoke. It was only 9.30pm when she put me to bed. It must have been some binge. I didn't wake up until 8.30 this morning. My mouth felt as if someone had ripped out my tongue and replaced it with carpet fluff. My head was throbbing so much I expected to be able to see it changing in size as I looked in the mirror. My reflection only added to my misery, as I had never been aware someone could look so close to death with a hangover. I called work and left a message on the voicemail. I was too ill to actually talk to anyone. Kathryn popped her head round my bedroom door before she left for work. She told me I was not ill and that I had no-one else to blame but myself.

'Personally I blame my therapist' was how I had replied. She just shook her head, blew me a kiss and left. I lay in bed for another two hours just looking at the ceiling, wondering if I would ever walk again! But at five o'clock I am outside my second home, watching the rain chasing empty crisp packets to the drain at the bottom of the road.

The commuters don't like the rain. It makes them all look grumpy. They huddle under their umbrellas, unable to walk too fast in case they are speared to death by someone else's umbrella. I like watching people with umbrellas in crowds. It is funny to see them trying to manoeuvre in small places, round lamp posts and past someone else with an umbrella. I take bets with myself as to whether they will lift their umbrella over the other person, lower it to let the other person over or just keep walking forward hoping they come through the other side pierce-free. I try to stay umbrella-free as much as possible as I only leave them on buses and lose them. It became too expensive to keep up.

The last of this set of commuters trudges past, trying unsuccessfully to button up his beige mac with one hand whilst carrying an umbrella with the other and holding his briefcase under his elbow. I follow him to the end of the shops and leave him fiddling and cursing quietly to himself. The car is parked directly outside number 57, pointing the opposite way to normal; it is usually parked pointing down the hill. This unnerves me a bit, but I'm not sure why. I suppose it has rippled my routine. Her voice says hello, the buzzer sounds and I push my way into the dry hallway of number 57. The red flowering plant has disappeared and has been replaced with a vase full of dried lavender. I preferred the red flowers.

The red door opens slowly and I smile at her, feeling like a puppy who knows he has done something wrong, but is not quite sure how to make it right again. She smiles back. The all-forgiving therapist.

'It's not as cold as you think outside,' I say, taking off my coat and jumper.

'You mean it's too warm in here?' she asks, sitting down in her chair.

'Yeah, something like that,' I laugh.

'Just bear with me a minute,' she says and leans forward picking up something from the floor. 'I forgot to switch the ringer off the phone.' It beeps a few times as she pushes a button on the handset. 'There, sorry about that.'

'That's OK.' I look down at the carpet and see that someone has trailed mud through. I look at my shoes and think that it was probably me. I think about apologising, but there is nothing I can do about it now. And anyway, it might not have been me, it might have been Mystery Client before me and then I'd just look as if I was paranoid and she'd only analyse the fact I felt I had to apologise, and she'd want to know what I was really apologising for. Then I realise that actually I probably should apologise for my behaviour yesterday, but then that would mean I did something wrong. But I did. It wasn't right. It *was* right. It was how I felt. What is so wrong with that?

'Can I be part of the conversation going on in your head?' she asks.

The argument becomes silent, like two naughty children, neither wanting to speak up first. She doesn't push the matter, but sits quietly and I can feel her watching me. I begin to fidget. And suddenly the strap on my watch seems awfully important. I must examine it. I sense the moment she sees the newest cuts, on the same arm as I wear my watch. Perhaps I really wanted her to see them, but I don't want to talk about them. So I launch into a heartfelt apology.

'I'm sorry for yesterday. I should have known better. I should not have turned up drunk.' In my head I'm on my knees in front of her, head hung low, looking at her shoes.

'I was disappointed that you didn't go to work. That you didn't do what would have helped you stay safe.'

My heart sank, put rocks in its pockets so it wouldn't surface again. She was disappointed in me.

'I'm sorry. I didn't go today either,' I say, mortally ashamed, as if it was the worst thing anyone could do.

'It is not me you need to apologise to. It is yourself. It makes no difference to me whether you go to work or not, but I can see that you're safer at work.' She makes complete sense and for a moment I hate her for that.

'I know.' I shake my head. 'I know, but sometimes it is so much easier to stay with this feeling than fight it. It can be really hard at work; it doesn't like being chained down. It needs to move and work gets in the way.'

'But isn't that a good thing?' she asks straightaway. 'Don't you want something that takes your mind off it all for a while?'

We stay silent for a while. Me thinking, her watching it all sink in.

'When did you cut?' Her voice is quiet, unobtrusive.

'Yesterday.' Almost a whisper. My eyes are closed. 'I wanted to show you how much I hurt; I wanted you to look after me.'

'Responsibility' is all she says.

'Huh?' I don't understand. 'Whose responsibility?'

'Exactly,' she says, trying to keep the smug therapist noise from her voice. 'It should be yours.'

'Mine? What should be mine?' I feel as if she is talking in Latin to me. Perhaps she has lapsed into 'Therapish', a language only therapists know. I sometimes feel as if she runs away with her own thoughts and leaves me at the wayside, thumbing a lift to try to catch up. I rub my hand over my forehead and bring myself back to the room.

'...and so you see it has to be you who takes the responsibility.'

I think I may just have missed an important speech. I search my brain to see if any part of it was listening. Nope, nothing. Whoops.

'Does that make sense?' she asks.

'Erm, well, yes, I guess so,' I say, not wanting to disappoint her, 'but do you think you could run it by me again, just to let it sink in.' Good call. I do a little victory dance in my head and try to stop myself thinking about a beach full of therapists, all hiding trash novels behind the covers of a Freud or Rogers.

She leans forward a little, pleased I'm taking this so seriously. 'OK, in simpler terms what I meant was that the responsibility for looking after you starts and ends with you. You need to be able to make the right choices for you, to help you stay within the real world.'

I nod. She's drawn me away from the beach and I know what she says is right. My adult mind knows that it was my choice to go and get drunk, to stay away from work.

'Asking me to take responsibility for you means that you can lay the blame on me every time you fall off the track. If you cut then it will be my fault because I wasn't there for you. If you end up outside where you consider me to live it will be my fault because I wasn't there to stop you. Do you see what I'm saying?'

'Yes, yes, I see completely. It makes sense, to part of me.'

'Yes, and to the other part of you, the Manipulator, it won't make sense because it doesn't want to know about responsibility.'

'That's exactly right.' I'm glad she understands. 'But it is this split that makes it very difficult sometimes.' I take a deep breath and let it out slowly as I try to form the right words in my mind to describe this properly for her. 'There is my adult side, my sane side; the part here at the moment who can understand things like that, who wants to get it right. Then there is the other side; what did you call it? The Manipulator, who just wants to be let loose and do all the things I shouldn't.'

'Be let loose into madness.' She carries on my train of thought as if she can read my mind. 'If you're mad then you have no responsibility, you can blame it on the madness, say you had no control.'

She passes the thoughts back to me. 'It is the pull between the two different sides that can be so hard. And yes, the idea of responsibility makes part of me reel back in disgust.' I throw the topic back to her as if the very thought of it is burning my mind.

She catches it, holds it carefully and says, 'The Manipulator is very strong. It is stopping you feeling about the rage inside you, a rage you might not even know about consciously. The Manipulator needs to be tackled.'

Chapter 16
Reflections

The journey home from therapy is just a haze. All I could think about was the Manipulator. It was easier to imagine now because it had a name. I could suddenly separate this part of me out and see it for what it was. But how long could I hold onto this, how long could I be stronger than it? I can't remember getting on a bus or walking to my front door, but I must have. I find myself in the bathroom looking in the mirror. I trace the line of my face on the glass.

I see a familiar face when I look in the mirror, one who has been around since I can remember. Things don't seem to change for the face. Still the blue eyes, still the questioning look asking, 'Who are you? I see you every day, but I don't know you.'

It feels as if we've never been properly introduced. We share the same space yet we feel so detached. We've spent an awfully long time avoiding each other. I feel that the reflection is waiting for the best moment to turn and run, run away from thoughts that seem to invade and don't belong.

I look in the mirror and sometimes the face looks so empty, sometimes I'm scared that it is me. There are photos of the face smiling and calm. Where did that person go? Did she ever exist? When I look at those photos I see only a face. Where are all the thoughts; why aren't they visible? Why can't I capture them in a photo and take the time to study them?

I want to peel away the face and look beyond. What is there? What does the Manipulator look for when it goes searching? Something to fill the void? To fill me? That word, 'me', a label so powerful, yet it means nothing when there is no identity attached.

A blank face staring out of the mirror waiting for a time when she is full, when she is not scared to say 'Hi' to the person looking back.

Chapter 17
Operation Bin

I step away from the mirror and close the bathroom door. I sit on the side of the bath and stare at the wall. I'd thought long and hard about the Manipulator when I left therapy. I'd thought so hard that I must have missed my stop because I had to walk an extra ten minutes to get home. But it gave me time to come to some conclusions.

The Manipulator is stopping me from really feeling what is happening for me. It wants to me to believe that I have to go out on cold nights, get drunk and stand outside someone's house. It wanted me to believe that I need to do this to feel better. But it isn't true. I think naming the Manipulator in therapy has frightened It off. It had been found out and now I couldn't feel It. It was hiding. I don't believe that talking about It just once can make It disappear for ever, but walking home last night I decided I had to take action whilst It is AWOL. I had tried to separate in my mind all the things I feel and do that could be due to the Manipulator. The main two were the cutting and the searching. But these things are like a barrier to what I really feel. The cutting stops me from feeling, makes me think of the pain on my arm. The searching makes me feel as though I am doing something useful, something proactive. Searching makes me feel no better, it doesn't achieve anything. It has to stop. I felt my heart beat hard when I thought this. I knew the Manipulator was still in there somewhere, listening to my thoughts. Perhaps It could feel the end coming nearer. Perhaps It could feel I was getting stronger. I certainly felt so right now. I felt as if I had the upper hand on this thing for the first time. And I wasn't going to let this opportunity go.

I stand up and look in the mirror at the face again.

'I feel I've let you down recently. I feel I've been running away from you. I'm sorry. I'm going to do something for you. For me.' I smile. This felt good. 'Come on then, let's go get 'em!' I open the bathroom door and walk into the kitchen with a flourish.

'Today is a good day,' I announce.

Kathryn jumps, spills her tea on her leg and looks at me suspiciously. She looks me up and down, her eyes narrowing. She thinks I've finally flipped, that I've handed myself over to the Manipulator completely. But no, I'm not going to let that happen.

'You OK, honey?' she asks, mopping the tea up with her dressing gown sleeve.

'Yup, do you know something, I think I am.' I breathe in deeply. 'But it might not last so we have to work quickly. Follow me.'

I grab her by the arm, spilling the tea again and pull her out of the kitchen. 'What the hell are you doing?' Kathryn giggles, 'You sound like you just fell out of a bad action movie.'

'Therapy tonight,' I explain badly, 'It was like a dawning. For the first time something made sense to me. Something I can grab and keep hold of. Something for me to control this whole bloody thing for once.'

'Ah right, I thought so,' she sniggers.

She sits down on the settee and watches in amazement as I go round the flat producing razor blades like some sort of macabre magician. She doesn't ask what I am doing or how many there are; she simply waits patiently for me to finish.

Before long there is a heap of blades on the coffee table, enough to keep a small scrap metal firm in trade for a month. I stand and look at the table, hands on hips, my breathing heavy. I can feel the Manipulator running round Its room banging on the walls, screaming, sensing what is going to happen. But It won't come out. It knows I am too strong right now. I am scared of the repercussions my next actions will have, but this has to happen. I have to show It that I mean business.

'Will you help me?' I ask, looking at Kathryn. She nods, but I can tell she doesn't actually know what I am asking of her. 'I want to throw them away.'

Then a door in my head clatters open and I feel the Manpulator storm to the front of my head.

You can't do this.
Think this through.
What are you going to do without them?
How are you going to show how much you hurt?
How am I going to control you?

'Are you sure about this?' Kathryn asks, leaning forward, looking concerned.

I close my eyes for a minute, ramming the door in my mind shut and hammering over some planks of wood as you see them do in cartoons.

'Yes,' I say firmly, 'this needs to be done and I want to do it now. It feels right.'

'OK,' she nods, standing up and tightening her dressing gown, 'Lead the way!'

I hold the blades in my cupped hands and we walk back through to the kitchen.

'I think we should wrap them in kitchen roll,' Kathryn suggests.

'What, like some kind of shroud?' I ask, wondering what the significance is.

'No, silly, so those scavenging cats don't hurt themselves when they rip open the bin bags.' She laughs and hands me a couple of sheets of kitchen roll.

I place the blades in the middle and wrap them up into a ball. She lifts the lid of the bin. 'Go on then, you do it.'

I drop the small white package into the bin and suddenly feel sick. Can I do this? I am beginning to doubt myself already. Kathryn puts her hand in the bin and pushes the package under all the other rubbish.

'There,' she says, 'now don't you go getting them back out.'

She sees the fear in my eyes and the tears beginning to well.

'I'm proud of you.' She holds her arms out to me. 'Give me a hug. You know you're my best friend and I'm always here for you. You can do this. That was a huge step. Just keep going with this.'

I bury my head in her shoulder and start to cry. Then I lift my head and smile at her. There are tears, but they are tears of relief. Kathryn pulls away gently and goes to put the kettle on. She opens the top kitchen cupboard and gets a chair so she can see right to the back. After a minute of rummaging around she produces a packet of unopened chocolate biscuits. She offers them to me as she dismounts from the chair and returns to making the tea. When she hears me laughing she turns round.

'What?' she asks, looking at me waving the packet of biscuits in the air.

'I see I'm not the only one who stashes things in secret places then,' I say accusingly.

'They are for emergencies or celebrations only, m'Lord,' she says bowing to me. 'And I think you'll find it is now *only* me who stashes things.'

I look at her and smile. I feel good, very vulnerable as if my defences are open, but it feels good all the same. I feel calm, too calm, like the eye of a storm, but I choose to ignore the ominous feeling.

Chapter 18
Silent scrawl

It takes me a long time to get to sleep that night but when I do I dream deeply. The wind belts the rain against my bedroom window. I feel sleep coming as I listen to the rhythm of the falling rain. Soon my unconscious begins to unravel the events of the day.

The room is filled with black writing on the walls. Most of the furniture has been thrown about and broken. A wooden chair remains intact. On the chair sits a very enraged-looking child; I can't see the face. The words on the walls don't make sense, but they're written with intense anger, bold and black. I feel scared watching this child sitting so quietly yet holding in so much emotion, but I can't tear my eyes away. I feel we've met before but I don't know where.

There is a wicker cradle in the corner of the room. There are baby toys all around the cradle. They are all new and have never been touched. This corner of the room is untouched. The wallpaper is a light orange and unwritten on. I can see the pattern of white rabbits and teddy bears. I walk towards the cradle. There is a thick sense of sadness in this corner of the room. The silence is overwhelming. The child in the chair begins to sob. I touch the cradle but I don't need to look inside to realise that the cradle is empty. I can feel the sadness and the emptiness flowing into my ears, into my head, down my throat and into my lungs. It is too much. The child on the chair is crying loudly now. It gets off the chair and walks towards me, arms held open and eyes streaming with tears. I don't like this. It is too much. I look for a door, a way out, but the writing covers everything and I see no escape.

I wake up with a jolt, my heart racing. I feel around at the side of my bed and switch on my lamp. I want to make sure this is my room and that I have woken up. I lie back down, then turn my pillow over as I realise it is damp with sweat. I look at the green walls of my bedroom, and try to calm myself.

'There is no black writing. There is no cradle and no crying child.' I repeat this over and over until I can feel my heartbeat slowing to something a little more normal.

I lean to the side of the bed again and pick up my notebook and pen. I need to write this dream down before it melts away into nothing, although I'm quite sure that I won't forget it. Something about it felt too real. It is too attached to me to be forgotten.

Chapter 19
Childish interpretations

The scruffy little cat balances on the fence post outside number 57, its collar hanging loosely around its scrawny, matted neck. I stroke its head and it looks at me with small dark eyes longing me to stay and be nice to it for a little longer.

'You are very sweet, but I can't stay here for ever, you know,' and with that I press the bell. The cat steps off the post and wobbles towards me on the top of the fence. It sits and looks at me again.

'Hello,' says the crackly voice.

'Hello,' I reply and push the door open. I turn round and see the cat straining her head to see inside the warm house. 'Sorry, sweetheart,' I say. 'You can't come in here.'

Shutting the door slowly I turn round to see the red door already open and her watching me, laughing.

'She's very sweet, isn't she?' she says, 'She's called Tiny. I saw her owners the other day and I asked them what she was called.'

'Tiny?' I say smiling, 'Very apt.' I walk past her, remembering to wipe my feet on the mat before continuing into the therapy room. The kitchen looks a bit untidy as I pass through. There is a newspaper on the side, a notepad and a couple of pens. A pile of papers and a phone book sit next to the sink, the draining board is full of cups drip-drying and a cloth hangs over the taps.

In the therapy room it becomes clear why the kitchen is a mess; she has obviously had a busy day. There are two folders lying by the side of her desk and some photocopied articles strewn underneath. A pad of paper sits on the desk and for once it is not blank, but full of writing and diagrams. I wonder what she writes about. I'd like to freeze time so I can step outside the frame and have a look at what she is working on. It never dawns on me to ask, but then again I know she wouldn't tell me. She'd only ask why I felt the need to know. I smile to myself as I throw my jacket on the floor and sit on the couch.

'You seem happy today,' she says straightaway, never one to miss anything. Sometimes I like this, it makes me feel safe, that even if *I* don't know what I'm feeling *she* will. But sometimes it unnerves me and I don't like the constant watching and observing. It makes me uneasy. But today it is OK, I'm happy and I'm ready to tell her why.

'Yeah, I am,' I say, getting comfortable. 'The last session was such an eye-opener.'

'Oh?' She often says this when she wants me to take things further, expand for her.

'Yeah. The whole Manipulator thing really hit a chord. I was able to see for the first time what you must have been able to see for ages. But it wasn't until you really shoved my face in it that I could see It for what it was.'

'You're still calling the Manipulator "It",' she points out, 'The Manipulator is part of you. You need to start owning this part of you. Take responsibility.'

I fold my arms. She hasn't even given me a chance to tell her about the ritual throwing away of the razor blades before having a go at me. But I know she is right.

'I know, I know I should. But that's quite scary. At the moment it is easier for me to say 'It', because I have only just identified It. One step at a time, eh?'

'Yes, OK,' she backs down. 'But I need to keep you aware of what this really is.'

I nod in agreement, but know that somewhere I still see the Manipulator as some sort of infiltrator, not really part of me.

'I threw my blades away,' I suddenly blurt out.

Silence.

The most important thing I've done since starting therapy and I get no response. I sit on my hands and lower my head.

Silence.

I can't stand it any longer, I have to tell her. I give a description of collecting the razors from around the flat and how I threw them away. I don't tell her about standing in front of the bathroom mirror.

'How did that make you feel?' she asks.

'Elated. Released. Relief. It needed doing.'

I can hear police sirens in the distance and a helicopter droning on in the background. I did feel elated and released. Now I'm not sure. And as soon as I feel this momentary doubt I can sense the Manipulator slowly opening the door and stepping out, stretching Its arms and yawning as if It has been sleeping for the last two days.

'And now?' she asks, reading my mind and my body language. 'How do you feel now?'

I take a deep breath and listen to the police siren, trying to picture how far away it is, seeing if I can pinpoint which road it is on, which house it is outside.

'Come back,' she says gently. 'Tell me how you're feeling about it right now.'

She knows this is difficult for me, to be able to say how I feel right here, right now. But she needs me to stay with her, to stop me sliding into my mind.

'Erm, I think I feel scared,' I try. 'I'm not sure I did the right thing. I know at the time I wanted to be able to stop the

Manipulator from cutting. To stop It… sorry…to stop *me* from cutting so I could show you how I feel, so you'd take care of me. I need to talk more about it, not cut more.'

'Well, that's good. It is good you took responsibility for that.' I can hear her writing something down or maybe she is just doodling. I'll never know. 'Just try to hold onto that notion of responsibility, because it is easy for you to drop. Be aware that throwing the blades away won't stop the Manipulator; you still need to be stronger than it.'

We stay silent for a while, my mind trying to hang on to responsibility. I hold it close and sometimes I understand things so clearly, but sometimes it just makes no sense, it is so alien. Then I remember my dream about the child and the empty cradle and the feeling of utter emptiness. I look at the clock; I have only been here 20 minutes. It amazes me how time is either slow or fast when in therapy. There are times when as soon as I have settled in it is time for me to go again. But today time is on my side.

I begin to tell her about the dream. She listens intently and jots things down as I tell her about the writing on the wall and the colour of the cradle. She doesn't interrupt me but lets my mind tell her what it needs to.

'I was scared of the child in the chair. And the feeling of nothingness and just knowing the cradle was empty was so real, I can feel it now.' My heart is beating fast, I need to curl up somewhere dark and hide myself from the world, make everything disappear.

I hear her take a breath and wait for her to speak.

'What comes to mind when you think about the baby that isn't there?' she asks steadily, sensing my anxiety.

I put my hands over my face and take a deep breath. My mind tends to go blank when she asks me direct questions, mainly because I know she is expecting an answer, she is expecting me to get it right and I always think I'll say the wrong thing. I recognise I should stop thinking like that. She's not here to judge me right or wrong. She's here to help me make sense of my head.

'I think of me.' I didn't know I was going to say that and I'm a little taken aback. I lower my hands from my face, aware she might not be able to hear my mumbling. 'I think of me. That's it. That's all I can think of.'

She lets me think for a while then says, 'Can you say more? What image do you have of yourself?'

This time I don't need time to think as an image comes flashing into my mind.

'Just me. On my own in a big space. It's very white, everything is white, and you can't see where the walls end or even if there is a floor. I'm just sitting there, cross-legged, on my own.' I'm beginning to feel tearful. I've never cried in therapy before, not properly, not so she'd notice, but I can feel it welling up.

'It doesn't sound very safe,' her voice soft and quiet, 'no floor, no walls. You don't seem very contained. What is holding you in?'

The image is still in my head and I'm beginning to feel very vulnerable. I want to hug myself and hold myself tightly. I am suddenly aware of my body and feel as if it has no boundaries, as if I might just fizzle out into thin air. But I don't know how to put this into words. All I can say, in a whisper, is: 'Nothing. Nothing is holding me in.'

'It is interesting that there are two children in the dream,' she says, bringing me back to the room. 'There is the child in the chair, who is obviously scared. And then the baby, or not, in the cradle. The child in the chair only starts crying once you move towards the cradle? Is that right?' she asks, wanting me to clarify the content of the dream.

'Yes, that's right. The child on the chair was very quiet until I walk to the cradle.' I think hard. 'And as soon as I realise the cradle is empty then the child in the chair is sobbing uncontrollably.' I feel a shiver go through me.

'I think the child might be the Manipulator,' she suggests, 'And I think it wants to be looked after. To be held. To be made safe.'

I'm holding something back. The piece of information needed to make sense of the dream is not forthcoming.

'The Manipulator wants to take you back, to let you be reborn, to be looked after and cared for, to have the unresponsibilty of childhood. But that can't happen. You're an adult now.' She says this firmly, making sure I take in and digest her words.

I glance at the clock. Two minutes. The time has suddenly run through my fingers; she still has things to say, but I'm ready to go. I've had enough and need to go and hide under my duvet.

'It sounds to me as if the child on the chair is the part of you who had to hold things together. Perhaps thrown into an adult world of emotion from a very young age, especially if we think about how young you were the first time your father was ill.'

I stay silent. This makes sense to me, but my head is too full, I need to scream.

'I'm not saying that's all it is about,' she continues, 'but it does seem to me that there is a strong feeling of being left alone as a young child.'

I stare at the curtains and clench my fists. My head hurts. I'm already putting my coat on when she says: 'It's time.'

When I get outside the little cat, Tiny, is still there, perched on the fence post. I don't stop to pet her though. I need to run and get away from the feelings that the session brought up. I need to feel the rain in my face soaking through my mind. I want to run so fast that my mind is blown inside out and all the stuff I don't understand just tumbles to the floor and is swept away by the wind.

Chapter 20

Rescue me

I turn the corner and run across the road without looking. I hear a driver beep the horn and a screech of tyres, but I don't look back. Terraced houses flank me on either side and I begin to realise I don't know where I am. I carry on running, trying to think which way I have just run or how long I have been running for, but I can't. My mind was too busy having a meeting without me to be able to concentrate on such insignificant things as direction.

Suddenly I stop. The Manipulator is hanging from my mind and is swinging Its legs in front of my eyes. I can't see anything and my head is spinning. I wanted to run away, to get away from the feelings, but now I'm panicking. The Manipulator has been shaken free and wants to take control. Do I have the energy to say no?

GO BACK.
TELL HER SHE NEEDS TO MAKE THIS BETTER.
TELL HER YOU CAN'T DEAL WITH THIS ON YOUR OWN.
THIS IS HER FAULT.
YOU NEED HER.
I DON'T WANT TO BE ON MY OWN.

'I don't want to be on my own,' I hear myself say out loud. 'Don't let me be on my own.'

Then the aching begins. It feels as if my heart is being pulled out of my chest. I'm frightened. I'm small again. Sitting in a white room all by myself. I need to search. I need to be near her. I don't want to be on my own; I don't like it here. I slump down on the pavement with my back up against a wall and sit for a moment with my head in my hands. Sitting still only makes it worse. I need to travel. I need to keep moving to stay one step ahead of this awful feeling. Standing up I turn round and begin to walk back the way I came. Back to therapy. Just to be near somewhere safe.

MAYBE SHE'LL RESCUE YOU.

'Maybe she'll rescue me.' No, I'm not strong enough tonight.

Turning the corner I see the row of shops and a small queue inside the Indian takeaway. There is a boy sitting on my bench eating chips from a white paper cone. Two pigeons hover greedily round his legs. I go to sit next to him, but I've worked myself into such a state that the smell of vinegar and hot fat turns my stomach. I stand across the road under a shop awning and look at the door of number 57. Tiny is no longer sitting guard on her post and I wonder for a moment whether she is somewhere warm or still out in the drizzle like me. I glance up the road as an engine starts and the lights of a transit van switch on. It is then that I notice the car is not there. There is a car-sized space just up from number 57. She's gone. Just left, if the car-sized dry patch on the road is anything to go by. I manage a smile as I think what a wonderful detective I would have made. The Manipulator is pacing in circles in my head getting more and more worked up. It seems to be occupied with something at the moment which is quite worrying as It doesn't seem to be telling me what It is planning. For now at least I feel a bit more clear-headed and make a quick plan whilst It is otherwise engaged. It doesn't want to go home yet so if I can get to a bus stop and at least make It feel as though It is going somewhere, that will be a start. There is a bus stop two blocks away on the main road, over the railway line, so I set off that way feeling glad to be heading for a dry place at last. Crossing over the railway bridge I get caught up in a late influx of commuters. I look at my watch and think that these people are either very conscientious or not very good at managing their workload. They all look extra weary. I start to count hats to take my mind off the Manipulator and the empty cradle and the white room with no floor. Woollen hats seem to be the flavour of the day for commuters, mostly black, which comes as no surprise. There are two baseball caps and one very strange-looking Stetson with a piece of rope tied round the edge.

The man with the Stetson waits at the bus stop too, along with a few of the other commuters, but most of them carry on walking towards the tube station and car park. A bus pulls up and I get on without taking any notice of where it is going. I climb upstairs and sit at the very back next to two teenagers who are sharing the earphones of a rather loud personal stereo. Although the traffic is quite heavy the bus keeps on moving, only stopping to let passengers off. Soon I am completely lost and the upstairs seats are nearly empty, apart from me and the two teenagers.

Then, crash. It wakes up.

WHERE ARE WE? LET ME SEE. WHERE IS THIS? WHY ARE WE HERE? I HAVE TO GO TO HER HOUSE; I HAVE TO GO THERE AND I HAVE TO GO THERE NOW. I NEED TO GO THERE, WE NEED TO GO THERE.
NOW!

I shake my head and slump down in my seat. I tried. I tried so hard to keep It happy, to travel and to keep moving, I've been trying to take responsibility for It but it is not good enough and now I don't know what to do. I could let It take over completely. Stick two fingers up to responsibility. It would be so easy.

Then the lights of the bus flash on and off and I know we have reached the last stop. I need to go home. I'm tired and don't trust myself out here. The Manipulator is pulling and I feel the aching feeling in my stomach getting stronger and I know I have to get home, to bed, with a cup of tea and the door shut, keeping myself safe. I get off the bus and go to look at the map of local buses. There are three that go near enough past my road to be helpful. There are also two that go past her road, which is not helpful, and I have to tear myself away from waiting for them to get on a bus that will take me home. The bus is quite empty and sails along quickly. I'm walking down my road within half an hour, the Manipulator cursing me loudly for not getting one of the other two buses.

I slam the front door and lean against the wall. All I can hear is the complaints and uproar of the Manipulator. I start to bang my head against the wall.

'Go away. Go away. Go away. Go away,' I say with every hit.

I jump when I feel a hand on my shoulder and open my eyes to see Kathryn standing in front of me.

'You don't want to be doing that, mate,' she says, eating an apple. 'You might damage the wall.'

I manage a smile, but it means nothing. I need to be on my own. I need to be somewhere dark. I walk past her and up the stairs, ignoring Cat, who tries to wrap himself round my legs as I pass. In the bathroom I splash my face with cold water and glance in the mirror. I see nothing and no one. Without thinking I grab a disposable razor and head for my room. With the curtains pulled and the small lamp on my chest of drawers switched on, I sit in the corner of my room and start to work at the disposable razor. I get a pen and manage to lift up the piece of plastic surrounding the blade. I wiggle the nib under a bit more and eventually there's a sudden snap and the plastic flies off somewhere underneath my bed. With one of my door keys I then prise the blade out of the rest of its holder. I've done this before, can you tell? I sit with the blade in the palm of my hand.

I KNEW YOU COULDN'T LAST WITHOUT THEM.
CUT ME ALL YOU WANT, BUT YOU WON'T CUT ME OUT OF YOUR MIND.

I hate It. I hate It so much. I don't want to cut but what else can I do? How else can I shut It up, numb It down?

I look down at my arm, focus my mind and ignore the storm in my head.
Blacker and blacker, anger implodes. Shut my eyes and clench my fists.
Fight the feeling. Or let it flow. Why can't I just be somewhere else?
Sitting cross-legged, head hung low. I can't hold it inside anymore.
I need to do this, I have to do it. Pick up the razor and feel the edge.
Arguments stop. The eye of the storm. Physical pain has words.
The aftermath.
Hate and shame.
Look away but keep watching.

I can hear Kathryn's television in the next room as I press hard on my arm with a tissue. The cut is deep. My legs are wobbly. I scared myself. It is bleeding a lot and this is my last tissue. I press as firmly as I can, taking deep breaths to calm myself. I try to think of mundane things to bring me down and decide to pick out a long-sleeved shirt to iron for work in the morning. My hands are shaking as I open my wardrobe and I sit on the side of my bed to stop my legs from buckling. The cut is really stinging now, but I know the Manipulator is pleased with it. There will be a good scar. I might be scared, but I can tell It is glad I'm scarred.

Chapter 21
A break too many

I was late for work this morning because I slept in. I'm usually tired for a few days after a night like that, but this time I was exhausted. Being crazy really takes it out of you.

My cut starts to bleed twice during the day and I have to go and rinse my arm under the tap in the kitchen area. It still stings like hell when I immerse it in water. But the pain keeps the Manipulator happy. Some of my colleagues go out together for lunch but I decline their offer. It's Barbara's birthday and they're splashing out on pizza. I just want today to end so I can get to therapy. I don't feel very sociable and anyway, despite getting up an hour late, I still managed to find time to make my own lunch.

There is an hour between finishing work and the start of therapy, loads of time, usually, so I catch a bus instead of getting the tube because I like watching London go by as opposed to the scenery-free Underground. But today this was a mistake. After 45 minutes of travelling by bus at walking pace I realise I am going to be late. When the traffic grinds to a halt altogether and I'm only half-way there I know that unless I get off and run I might not ever get there. Being destined to sit on a 143 bus for the rest of my life is not good. A queue of people wait impatiently in the doorway to get off the bus as the doors hiss and slide open. We all pile off. Dodging the puddles as I run and keeping an eye on the traffic, I pass four other buses stuck in the traffic. I look at my watch; five minutes till six o'clock. I'm never going to make it; surely my lungs will burst before I'm anywhere near number 57. The crossroads ahead means I'm not too far away and it is all downhill from here, apart from the last steep hill up to the railway station and the steps up to cross the bridge, that is. The traffic lights are at green as I come to the crossing, but the traffic is so slow that I manage to cross without any problems. The run downhill is a blessing, although my knees are getting wobbly again, but this time from exhaustion. Running up this last hill in normal circumstances would be difficult, so after running non-stop for 15 minutes beforehand it's an impossibility. I stop at the bottom and catch my breath, but only for a moment. I'm nearly there now; I might be too out of breath to talk to her but at least I'll be there.

I literally fall onto the doorbell and wheeze hello when she answers. I collapse onto the couch and sit there breathing heavily whilst she gets settled.

'Sorry I'm late.' I wipe sweat off the back of my neck. 'Bloody traffic. I had to run here from Finsbury Park.'

'Oh dear. Would you like a glass of water?' she asks, sounding sincerely concerned.

'Yes,' I rasp, 'yes, if that would be OK.'

She leaves the room and I hear her opening a cupboard and running the tap. I lean forward and put my hand up the back of my shirt. I'm dripping with sweat, not hugely attractive. I roll the sleeves of my shirt up, see my cut glaring up at me and roll them down again. But I'm too hot, so roll them up and keep my arms by my side as she comes back in and gives me the glass of water. I sip carefully, although what I really want to do is tip it over my head and feel it run down my back. I go to run my hands through my hair then put my arm quickly back down my side. But in therapy world the cut has already been noted and she says:

'So, tell me about how you've been since we last met.'

My breathing has calmed down now but my cheeks are hot and flushed. 'Awful,' I say, 'absolutely bloody awful.'

'Can you tell me about it?'

I take another sip of water. 'I don't know where to start,' I laugh.

'Start wherever you like,' she says. 'Keep it simple, don't let it get stuck, just say what happened then we'll move onto feelings if that makes it easier for you.'

I put the glass on the carpet and look up at the ceiling. 'OK,' I say taking a deep breath. 'As soon as I left after the session I wanted to run as fast as I could away from here. That is so different from usually wanting to hang round, but I just ran and ran and then I didn't know where I was and I panicked and all of a sudden I had to come back.' I close my eyes tightly, trying to remember what it felt like. I'm sure it doesn't make sense to her when I talk about it. Describing how I felt is so hard; I just had these feelings and that was it. Feelings don't have words. That is why they are called *feelings*. Take pins and needles for instance. I only know what I feel is pins and needles because I have heard other people describe it, but because I can't feel their pins and needles I will never know if what I am feeling is the same as what they are feeling. Or yellow, take yellow for instance. How do I know that what I see as yellow is the same as what you see?

It is at this point that I unscrew my head and throw it into the waste paper basket, but I can still hear myself from there.

Then there is the strong urge I have to justify my feelings (and my actions during these feelings) to her, but that is silly and I have to stop doing it. Then I get myself stuck between needing to talk but not wanting to justify things and wanting to say the right thing so I'm pleasing her and, oh, this is so hard. Things would be so much simpler without feelings. I grab my head out of the basket and shake it.

'You're doing it again,' her voice says, shattering my thoughts, 'You are shaking your head, stop editing and let me in.'

'I was just thinking how much easier it would be without feelings.' I laugh, wondering whether I should tell her I just unscrewed my own head. 'I feel as though I need to justify what I feel, to ask you if I'm doing things right.'

'Yes, I know you find that difficult. But you need to stop assuming there is a right and a wrong. We're here to understand *why* you do things and not to judge.' She sounds fed up. 'Remember what I said about keeping it simple. The more you think about something the more complicated you make it.'

My first instinct is to clam up and sulk because I feel she has told me off; I take it as a negative, but I know this is not useful. 'OK, simple things. OK, I can do this.' I rub my face with both my hands and stare at the curtains. 'I came back here, don't know why, I just needed to. But your car was gone and that made me want to go to your house, but I knew I shouldn't so I just got on any bus to make myself feel as though I was going somewhere, but it didn't really work and when I got home I cut. I cut really badly and I scared the hell out of myself and I feel so bad for doing it because I'd thrown my blades away and thought I was ready to beat this thing.'

'But you didn't come to my house. That was good, wasn't it?' She points out the positive that I'm blindly avoiding.

'Yes, I guess so. But, oh, it was so hard. I had to struggle with myself and argue and fight.' I can feel the anger welling up in the pit of my stomach and I draw my legs up and hold my arms around my knees. 'I felt so alone, as if I was in the white room again and I didn't want to be there. I sat on the pavement in the rain for God's sake. I wanted to disappear there and then and just end this whole thing. Shit, I don't understand how I can just flip like that.' I bury my head between my knees and hope that the world ends soon because sometimes I've just had enough.

'Don't disappear.' Her voice is tender and soothing. 'You have too much to offer the world yet. There is so much potential there to show everyone. Don't let it disappear.'

'I'm just so tired of it all,' I mumble from between my knees.

'Yes, it can be exhausting, but no one ever said therapy was going to be easy.' She clears her throat and I sense an important speech looming. 'I want you to imagine a piece of thread, because I think that's what it feels like for you, as if you are hanging by a thread. I think it is that precarious for you. But I'm holding on to one end of that thread and as long as you don't let go of your end this will be OK. It is up to you, however. I won't let go of my end but you need to keep hold of yours.'

She stays silent whilst the image settles in my mind. I picture a piece of string tied to my wrist and the other end to hers. And I like that. It makes me feel safe. A lifeline. I wonder how long this piece of string can stretch. I imagine it unweaving all over London as we move about in different places and I like that too. After all, a piece of string is as long as it needs it to be and I know that if I feel bad I can follow it all the way back to her. I'm not sure if she meant it like that and I'm not going to ask just in case she didn't, but I find the image comforting and I'm going to hold on to it.

Then she says, 'I think one problem that you have is that you don't believe I can hold you in my mind when you're not here. You don't think it is possible for you to be remembered unless you are here. It's as if you need my approval and when I'm not around you panic and need to find me so you can find yourself.'

Exactly! She is spot on. But again how can I know she is thinking of me or remembering me when I'm not there? I'm not there. I don't know what she is thinking when I am here let alone when I'm not. I don't say this out loud though, as I know I am not keeping things simple enough. This time I unscrew my head and put it in the plant pot at the other side of the room, hoping the dirt will smother anything else I've got to say.

'Well, if you're holding tightly to your end of the rope I have something to tell you,' she says brightly, too brightly. The ominous feeling of bad news leaks into the air. I bury my head further under the soil. 'In two weeks' time I have a conference to go to and won't be here for the week.'

I automatically stop breathing and grab the sides of the couch. I think I'm going to die. The overwhelming feelings of abandonment and jealousy and anger grab hold of my stomach and curl it into knots.

'Obviously I won't charge you for the sessions you'll miss, but I need to tell you now so we can work out how it will make you feel having an unscheduled break, especially as it is so close to my normal break at Christmas.'

Two mentions of a break in one sentence. If I thought I was capable of standing I would have thrown open the red curtains, smashed my fist through one of the windows, grabbed a shard of glass, drawn it down my forearm and thrust the cut into her face.

'How does it make you feel, me telling you that?' she asks, unaware of my head in the plant pot and my arm shredded by the glass from her window.

'OK, I guess,' I lie and suddenly I'm transported to the white room.

The room is large and white. At second glance there is a row of chairs around the wall, but I'm the only person sitting in the room. The chairs are brown and plastic and each one has a hole in the back the shape of a letterbox. I must be quite young because my feet don't reach the floor and I am swinging my legs back and forth slowly. There is no one else here. In the middle of the room is a table strewn with magazines, all old and tatty. Other things begin to blur into focus and I can see posters on the white walls. I stand on my chair and look at one of them above me. It has a picture of a cigarette and a heart on it. The heart has a face drawn on it and it looks very sad. There are lots of long words I don't understand but I can read the bottom line that says that smoking kills. It doesn't say what it kills, just that it kills.

I sit back down on my chair and swing my legs again. I feel as if I have been here a long time. People in white coats and green uniforms keep popping their heads round the door. I ignore them because they keep asking if I'm OK, and I don't know who they are or why they should need to know that. So I don't look at them. I pretend they are not there. Then they go away again and I'm on my own which, although it is very scary because I don't know where I am, is better than having them looking at me.

And then the door opens again and a woman walks in. She is not wearing a white coat or a green uniform, just normal clothes. She looks as if she's been crying because her eyes are black where her makeup has run. She is carrying a paper cup full of coffee. I know this because I can smell the bitter smell that reminds me of my mum making a pot full of coffee for my dad to take to work in his flask. Then she asks me the question that I haven't known the answer to for all these years until now:

'What are you doing by yourself in here sweetheart?'

'I'm waiting for my mummy to come and get me.'

And I'm back in the therapy room with tears rolling down my cheeks and I have my arms round my knees and I'm rocking backwards and forwards. I put my left hand down to the side of the couch where I know there is a box of tissues waiting for such events. I've never needed it before and I'm embarrassed to be taken unawares like this. I hold the tissue over my face and try to compose myself.

'Can you tell me where you have just been because you don't seem very OK?' she says unobtrusively, knowing that I might not want to tell her what just made me let go for the first time in a year of therapy.

'Oh, God, that was weird. The white room, you remember the white room?' I ask, my head now out of the plant pot, very firmly back on my shoulders, trying to make sense of all that just happened in my mind.

'Yes, the one without a floor or walls?' she replies, 'Go ahead, say more.'

I tell her about the posters, the chairs, my swinging legs, the nurses in uniforms, the smell of antiseptic and the way I thought I'd been forgotten about because my mum didn't come back to get me for a long time.

'And no one would tell me what was going on,' I continue, wiping my eyes with another tissue, holding the other one tightly in my clenched fist. 'I knew I was there because of my dad but they wouldn't tell me why. They didn't think I would understand, but kids can tell things, you know, they know when things are not right. They can sense stuff.'

'So you felt as if they didn't take you seriously?' she asks, trying to dig deeper.

'Yeah, that's right. They just left me there. When all I needed was for someone to tell me what was happening. They just thought I would get in the way. My brother was in on it all because he is older, but not me. Shut me in a room and hope I don't get out. That's what it was like.'

She stays silent and I want someone to hold me to stop me from being this scared.

'I need to cut,' is all I can say.

'Well, you're in here with me so you can't cut,' she says firmly, knowing that my last statement means my head needs to shut down. 'I've been thinking about a way that we might be able to make the forthcoming breaks easier for you, something to help keep you safe, free from the risk of harming yourself and to stop you going to the places we've talked about you not going to.'

I sit up and sniff. 'OK, sounds interesting. Go on, tell me.'

'A contract,' she says simply.

Chapter 22
Fruit bowl stuff

'A contract,' I repeat, not a question but a statement, letting the words settle into my mind.

'Yes, a set of rules between us that we will both stick to. And it is important that this is a two-way contract with rules for me as well as yourself.'

'Like what?' I ask, not really understanding her.

She stops to think for a while. 'I think it should be something you take away with you and think about. Like homework.' She laughs. 'I need to know that you will stop going to where you think I live. That has to stop. It has been a valuable experience for me to come through this with you, but now it has to stop. And I want to be able to trust you that it can stop and also you need to have something in place so you can trust yourself.'

'Wow, you've really thought about this, haven't you?' I say, quite chuffed that she has been thinking about me outside of our therapy time. 'But, yeah, I understand what you mean. Something to put the trust back into therapy, yes?'

'That's right, yes, do you think you can do that for next time?'

'I don't see why not,' I say and look at the clock. 'I'll brainstorm it and see what seems important to me.'

Our time is up and I feel as if I've been sitting on a roller coaster for the last 50 minutes, but I feel positive. I have something to work on that will keep me contained yet something that involves us both. I touch my wrist and think of the thread and hold on to it tightly as I walk out into the dark evening.

All the way home I think about the thread getting longer and longer, leaving traces over North London. I imagine cars getting caught up in it, people stepping over it, but it doesn't break. I imagine her being able to reel me in if I stray somewhere I ought not to. I imagine her holding the thread even when I'm not in a session and that makes me smile. If she can keep a hold, so can I. As I shut the door I hear Kathryn shouting a greeting and step over Cat who is intent on tripping me up as he hurtles down the steps. The smell of cooking lingers in the kitchen and I see a pile of onion skin, pepper cores and aubergine ends on the table. I sweep these into my hand and put them in the bin.

'I'm not your bloody mother, you know, tidying up after you.' I raise my voice just enough so Kathryn will know she's done wrong, again.

I hear a mumbled apology come from the living room as I sit down at the kitchen table with notepad and pen. I sit there for ten minutes staring at the fruit bowl, not knowing where to start.

'OK, a contract, a Therapy Contract,' I write at the top of the paper and underline it twice. 'So, what is this all about? What do I need a contract for?'

Under the title I write, 'A contract is needed to:' Then I doodle a smiley face in the margin and a dog sitting next to a tree. Then my brain kicks into gear and I get the first part written without much trouble:

A contract is needed to:

- stop me from putting myself at risk (and maybe being thrown out of therapy)

- stop the searching and 'stalking'
- help me to keep things real and take my feelings into therapy
- put the trust back into therapy.

'Sounds easy,' I say to the fruit bowl, 'Now for the hard bit. What am I going to agree to in this contract? I don't want to make it too hard on myself; I need to be able to stick to it.'

I hear Kathryn walk out of the living room, trip over Cat, who likes to sleep stretched out on the top step, and head for the kitchen.

'Who you talking to?' she asks, pulling up a chair.

'The fruit bowl,' I say.

'Ah right, should have known.' She picks out an apple and rubs it on her jeans. 'What you talking to the fruit bowl about?'

'Oh, you know, just fruit bowl stuff.' I pull the pad closer to my chest.

'Mind my own business, right?' she says, getting up. 'If you find that the fruit bowl gets bored I'll be watching trash TV in the living room. So if you do want to talk please make an appointment because it is imperative I learn how to decorate my curtains with stencils.'

We both laugh. 'Actually...' I hesitate, drawing circles on the pad. 'I was wondering if I could ask you something.'

She sits back down again. 'Hey, you don't need to ask, go ahead.'

'I have to do a contract for therapy, you know, something that will help me take it in there and not wander round North London for hours on end.' I rub at my thumb where there is a spot of ink. 'And I wanted to know whether I can call on you if

I feel impulsive or need to cut. To see if I can stop it before it happens.'

'That's what I've wanted you to do anyway, stupid,' she says playfully, 'but I guess you had to realise yourself that that is the way to go.' She takes a bite out of the apple and looks at me thoughtfully. 'Anytime, you should know that already. You have to listen to me often enough about my woes, so of course, and let's face it, I'll be more help than a bloody fruit bowl.'

I giggle. 'Oh, you are a star. I think I just needed to ask, so now I know there is no excuse for me not asking for help. Before it was easy to think that you'd be busy or not want to, but now I've asked it will feel easier. And yes, the fruit bowl was beginning to look rather uninterested.'

'OK, show me the contract when you've done if you like. But for now my curtain show is calling, got to go!' and she bustles out of the kitchen, taking another apple with her. I have never known anyone eat as much fruit as Kathryn.

For the next hour and a half I sit at the kitchen table. My doodles get larger and the fruit bowl is still no help, but I end up with two lists, one under the heading: 'By agreeing to this contract I will' and the other list under: 'In return, my therapist will'. The second list is shorter but just as important in my eyes. I decide not to show Kathryn what I have come up with, but will type it up more neatly at work in the morning and then take it with me to my next session.

At the office the next day, in between emails and real work, I type up the contract. Each time I read it, it seems to reinforce my feeling that this will work, this will make the difference. This will help me to keep things in therapy and be able to get on with a normal life. I read the contract over and over and see that I have been given some responsibility and for once I am going to do the right thing.

A contract is needed to:

- stop me from putting myself at risk (and maybe being thrown out of therapy)

- stop the searching and 'stalking'

- help me to keep things real and take my feelings into therapy

- put the trust back into therapy.

By agreeing to this contract I will:

- endeavour to talk openly about feelings and impulses rather than acting on them

- go straight home after therapy – *no hanging around*

- speak with my flatmate when I feel at risk of deeply cutting myself or feel impulsive when out on my own

- learn to focus on the 'real' when I am not in therapy

- not set myself up to fail or put myself in situations where it is going to be difficult to control the urge (e.g. drinking four pints on an empty stomach)

- be responsible for my own actions.

In return, my therapist will:

- encourage me to talk, rather than keep things secret

- understand and recognise that I might find it hard to stop and that the thought of stopping makes me panic inside

- remind me of the consequences if in any doubt that I am in danger of breaking the contract

- help me recognise when I am doing well.

I'm nervous about showing it to her because I know this is it. This is where I start taking control. The Manipulator is howling in my head. It doesn't understand why It needs to be contained, controlled. I can feel It stomping about, giving me a headache, making my head throb. But I'm relieved that things are going to change, I'm relieved that I'm feeling positive, however nervous I might be at the same time. I feel I can do this and, like the thread, I need to cling on to the feeling.

The sky is white and ominously full of snow as I wait for the bus after work. It was a clear, crisp blue sky when I left the flat this morning so I didn't think to bring an umbrella. They'd been threatening snow for days on the weather forecasts, but nothing had happened and I didn't actually believe it would. But the sky laughs down at me as I sit on the bus and it begins to sleet. The day gets darker and the sleet quickly turns into snow. Great big snow flakes, like I used to try to catch on my tongue as a child, fall to the ground. At first it doesn't stick, but soon all I can see out of the bus window is a sheet of white. If it carries on like this London will grind to a halt within the hour but I should be nice and warm in therapy before then. Getting off the bus into the freezing cold wind and snow isn't pleasant, but I trudge my way up the hill, pulling my scarf tighter round my neck. By the time I'm outside number 57 all I need is a carrot and two lumps of coal and I could easily pass as a snowman. I ring the bell and shake off as much snow as I can before pushing open the door and leaving a white trail behind me as I walk into the therapy room.

'You might want to think about going home, you know,' I say, taking off my coat and standing in the middle of the room, dripping. 'The roads are really icy and there are abandoned cars all over the place.'

'Oh dear, that doesn't sound good.' She takes my coat and lays it over the radiator. 'Are you OK?'

'Yeah, I'm fine, just cold,' I say, rubbing my hands together. 'But it won't take me long to defrost.' I take the contracts out of my pocket, unfold them and pass her a copy. 'Just see what you think; I can change things if you like, but I think it seems to cover everything and I wanted to make it realistic and...'

'Hey, sit down and relax. Let me read it!' She laughs, taking the piece of paper from me. She reads it out loud which makes me cringe, but I remember the last letter I gave her and how I hadn't known which bit she was reading and feel a bit better. At least this isn't full of gushing remarks.

'I was going to add a bit at the bottom about you supplying biscuits once a week when I have stuck to the contract, but I didn't think you'd agree to that,' I say when she has finished.

'You thought right,' she says straightaway, 'But this is good. I'm very pleased you've thought about it and thank you for doing this. I appreciate it. How do you feel about it?'

'Weird,' I reply without hesitating.

'Can you unwrap that word a bit more for me?' I hear her place the contract on the desk and her chair creaks as she sits back.

'Erm...' I picture the word in my head. I lift the top half of the word off and look inside. I can see lots of other little words inside that make up the meaning. I put my hand inside and pull a few of them out. 'Nervous, excited, worried and vulnerable all at once.' I close the lid on 'weird'.

'That's understandable,' she says reassuringly, 'but this is good and I think if we both work together and stick to the terms it will get easier. What are you most worried about?'

'The Manipulator.' And at the sound of Its name I feel the pounding in my head begin again. 'I don't trust It.'

'You need to leave that part of you in here. That's the part of you that doesn't belong out there.' The pounding gets harder. 'You have to trust me to keep It safe and that It is not too much for me. You think you're too much for me, that I can't cope, but trust me.'

I reach into my head, into the room with the writing on the walls and grab hold of the Manipulator. It struggles and whines, but I have a strong grip. I drag It out of the room, out of my mind and throw It into the corner of the therapy room. It sits there, stunned, looking back at me. We're face to face for the first time.

'I'll leave It in the corner,' I whisper hoarsely. 'I need to leave It here because I know It has been planning things since you mentioned the break. I know It wants me to break the contract and I can't do that. I need to move on.'

If I had turned round I would have seen a smile on her face, a smile that told me she knew for once I was telling the truth and that she trusted me. 'Well, I'm pleased about that and I won't let It out of this room. As long as It doesn't eat my plants, it can stay where It is and hopefully just join us during the sessions.'

I look over to the corner and It is cowering behind the curtains. I suddenly feel an aching inside and want It back. But I know it is a trick because as soon as I feel the first pang of doubt It looks out from behind the curtain with a glint in Its eyes. I swallow my doubt and It slinks back into the corner and begins to pick threads from the curtains.

'It'll be OK,' I almost chuckle, 'but you might want to keep an eye on the curtains.'

I turn round and she looks at me with raised eyebrows.

'Don't ask!' I laugh. 'I think I might go and see my mum when you're on your break. Keep me out of trouble.'

'That's a good idea,' she agrees, 'Let's start as we mean to go on.'

Chapter 23
All change

The last session before the break was hard and I knew it was going to be difficult to leave. But I managed. I left the Manipulator rummaging through the litter basket. It looked quite happy which felt good and I felt much lighter walking out of the door. She smiled at me and told me to take care of myself. I wished her a good conference and left, trying to ignore the aching feeling in my stomach. I cried myself to sleep, feeling very scared and alone. Kathryn was still in bed when I was ready to leave for the train station this morning. There was a note on the kitchen table from her telling me to have a good time and to call her whenever I needed to. I knew I would call if I needed to; she was easy to talk to. Cat was still an integral part of the family, but no longer my only comfort when I was down. Kathryn also said she hoped I wouldn't stay away too long or the kitchen would be under a mountain of vegetable peelings by the time I returned. I left her a note in return that I knew would make her laugh:

To Kat and Cat

Please note how clean and tidy I have left the kitchen.

Cat, your bowls are nice and shiny with no food dried to the side. Wash them when they are empty.

Kat, your bowls are also nice and clean and neatly stacked in the cupboard above the sink (the silver bowl shape with taps).

Cat, I changed my duvet cover yesterday. Please do not shed any fur on it.

Kat, the table is clear of all foodstuffs. Any vegetable peelings should be picked up and put into the grey cylindrical object next to the door. This is the bin. Fruit cores can also be placed in here.

Be good and see you soon!

Then I left and went to wait for a bus to take me to Kings Cross Station. I was looking forward to going up to see my mum and my brother and his kids. I'd phoned her two nights ago and told her I was coming up. She sounded surprised, but a nice surprised, as if she wasn't expecting to see me for a long while yet. She asked me how I had been and how come I never return her calls. I felt guilty. I always feel guilty when talking to my mum, as if something happened a long time ago that I've never been forgiven for. Or maybe it's a long-lost something I've never forgiven her for. I'm not sure, I don't remember, only the remnants of feelings remain. I often feel she is waiting for something, holding something back. Maybe one day the floodgates will open, but for now the phone call remains stilted.

I didn't mention my therapy or the cutting. I told her I'd been run off my feet at work and just been really tired. She didn't believe me, but she never said so. I could picture her fiddling with her blonde hair or playing with the glasses she keeps on a chain round her neck. I imagine her catching hold of my lie, folding it up and putting it in her pocket along with the others I've told over the years, lies I thought would protect her, from what I'm never sure. The atmosphere was already starting to build. There is so much that goes unsaid between me and my mum. We can sit together in a room, wordless, but the air surrounding us is full of feeling and unspoken truths. You have to sit very still or the words will hit you and find their way into your mouth, ready to be spoken. As a child I always sat very still, looking like a good, quiet girl. No one knew I was simply avoiding words.

Looking back, I can see that when I was small my dad was her first priority; she was worried, and she had other things on her mind. I was very good at being good, at being no trouble, at keeping out of sight. Suddenly I can remember watching her – I must have been about five – and concentrating hard, hoping to suck out all her hurt with my mind, so there was space for me. Just small enough for me, no one else, no worries, no fears. I'd curl up all safe and warm. I'd then feel guilty for wanting that space and even now, at 27 and a half, I can feel that guilt. It made me take a step back from her and that's where I've always been, a step away, not wanting to intrude, but desperately needing to. But I don't say this over the phone; I tell her I love her and give her my train times. She says she will make me my favourite meal, I tell her I'm looking forward to being looked after. And I mean this. There is no lie here. The five-year-old is reaching out, but not far enough, the void is too wide. It still feels strange being there without my dad, but without the Manipulator in the way I am hoping to be able to set some things to rest, but we'll see, no pressure.

The train is quiet for a Saturday and I have a table all to myself. I stretch and put my feet on the seat opposite, watching London go by. I like to watch London change from expansive city to neat suburbs and then finally to countryside. It reminds me that there is an escape from the city which is closer than you remember when you are trawling through the streets with a million other people. After a while all you can see are fields and the odd farmhouse and dilapidated-looking barn. Landscapes reel by but soon I don't see them. A cinema screen has been pulled down in my mind and a film is playing, blinding my open eyes to anything else.

There are three people sitting at a table: one is you, another is the therapist who sits in the out-of-bounds room and the third has a blank face but I feel that I know her. The room is in my parents' house, the house I grew up in, a square semi-detached house like all the others on the sprawling estate. I'm summoned into the room and sit on a chair at the opposite side of the table. It feels like a job interview, but I know you can see through me. I know you can read my mind. The woman with the blank face unnerves me and I fidget on the plastic chair. It reminds me of the ones in the white room. The ones that make a screeching noise on the floor if pushed about.

You're all here to ask me questions. The inquisition. I start to sweat and my breathing gets faster. I feel guilty but have yet to be tried. You're here to find out something. I look for the exit. You smile at me to put me at my ease. It doesn't work.

Outside the train window a lake floats past. Three swans and two cygnets sail by. The sun glints on the water and one solitary cloud hovers overhead, but my open eyes are still blind to all this.

I look at you across the table, my eyes pleading with you to make me feel better. And I suddenly understand the huge responsibility I place on you, how much I depend on you to make things right. And in that moment, if only for a second, I realise that you can't do this. You are there to help me understand, but it is up to me to do the rest of the work. The woman with the blank face asks me something. I'm not going to answer her; I only want questions from you. Why are you letting her ask me questions? I rise from the chair knocking it backwards and dash out of the room. I want you to follow, bring me back, make it OK. But you don't, you won't. I'm on my own in a hallway; there are a lot of doors in front of me. I have to choose which door to go through. They all look the same. The wallpaper is the same as at my parents' house, but there are too many doors. Too many doors and you are not here to guide me. My choice. My responsibility.

Fields upon fields upon square fields race past the train window. In one, a huddle of sheep idly watches the train pass by. In another there are two burnt-out cars and a lonely-looking horse. My eyes stare at all this but my mind sees none of it. My eyes see only doors. Large wooden doors.

I look behind me, to the door to the room of the inquisition, and want to go back in. But I know I can't do that, I've stepped over a threshold and there is no going back. There is no way I can de-understand something. It is scary, knowing that the responsibility for my choices and my life lies with me. Just me. I feel my stomach doing somersaults. Nothing behind these doors can be so scary. I repeat this over a few times and then I know which door I have to go through. I step towards it and the other doors fade away. The door behind me remains visible and I know this means that you won't leave me, you'll still be there to ease me through this new understanding until it becomes second nature. I feel a little relief. I'm not ready to give you up completely just yet. Knowing you are behind me, egging me on, I open the door in front of me. It is quite dark inside; there are curtains drawn and it takes a few moments for my eyes to adjust. There is a bed, covered with a purple duvet. A long lump in the bed suggests that there is an occupant. I walk slowly towards the bed, the anticipation and adrenalin mixing up in my stomach. I stand by the bed but the person doesn't stir.

Silence.

No, wait, I can hear breathing. The deep, slow breaths of someone deeply asleep. I stand there for a while unsure what this means. Then the lump moves, and coughs and sits up.

Dad.

I feel the longing and aching rising up from my toes, up through my legs, circling my stomach, pulling at my heart and clouding my head.

Farmhouses flash by, blurs of cows and tractors. I see nothing but my dad sitting in bed looking back at me.

I touch my wrist and feel the thread there. I tug it and feel some resistance. I know you are on the other end. I hold on tightly. I know that the searching has always been about this. Even when he was alive I was so scared of his death, always searching for him even when he was in front of me. The words 'I miss you, Dad' rise in my throat.

I'm back on the train, looking around, I'm not sure whether I spoke out loud or not. Nobody looks at me. Everyone is wrapped up in their own journey. I look out of the window and see the fields rolling away as far as the horizon. The snow has melted and the sky is winter blue. I think of therapy and of responsibility and of the Manipulator shredding the curtains, but at least I'll get to see the garden again. I'll be able to watch the squirrels chasing the birds away to get at the bread left out for them. With the Manipulator out of my head I can think much more clearly. The contract is folded neatly inside my wallet, to be carried with me at all times. I know that my own journey is not ready to come to an end yet, but perhaps it is time to change trains.

Further information and support

American Psychoanalytic Association, USA
309 East 49th Street
New York
NY 10017
Tel: (212) 752-0450

Guild of Psychotherapists, UK

The Guild is a professional and training organisation for psychoanalytic psychotherapists. The Guild offers a psychotherapy referral service for private psychotherapy.

47 Nelson Square
Union Street
Blackfriars Road
London SE1 0QA
Tel: 020 74013260
http://www.guildofpsychotherapists.org.uk

LifeSIGNS, UK

Self injury guidance and network support.

http://www.lifesigns.org.uk

National Mental Health Association, USA

The USA's oldest and largest nonprofit organisation addressing all aspects of mental health and mental illness.

2001 N. Beauregard Street, 12th Floor
Alexandria
VA 22311
Tel: (800) 969-NMHA (6642)
http://www.nmha.org

National Self-Harm Network (NSHN), UK

UK-based but available to everyone from any country. A survivor-led organisation supporting survivors and people who self-harm.

PO Box 7264
Nottingham NG1 6WJ
http://www.nshn.co.uk

SAFE Alternatives (Self-Abuse Finally Ends), USA

Committed to helping people achieve an end to self-injurious behaviour.

http://www.selfinjury.com

Young People and Self-Harm, UK

Information resource for young people who self-harm, their friends and families, and for professionals working with them.

http://www.selfharm.org.uk

Lightning Source UK Ltd.
Milton Keynes UK
UKOW05f0135040417
298280UK00001B/19/P